SHADES
OF GREEN
AND RED

Rod Lucas

Some recollections
from a Country Bus Driver
and Chiswick Works Engineer

Capital Transport

First published 2006

ISBN 185414 301 8

Published by Capital Transport Publishing
PO Box 250, Harrow, HA3 5ZH

Printed by Thomson Press
Lyon Road, Harrow, HA1 2AF

Title page Leatherhead garage had many ANs. Here is the author with
AN 43, one of the two-door variety, at Castle Road, Epsom.

Cover top Leatherhead garage when still under National Bus Company ownership.
On view is a BN blinded for a trip for Box Hill. The lady standing in the road is
waiting for the driver of the BL on the 71 to return from his break, as they had a
habit of not stopping at the first stop, the one outside the garage. *Ian Pringle*

Cover bottom The entrance to London Transport's Chiswick Works in April 1978 at
a time when vehicle shortages caused the hiring of preserved buses like RT 1400
(right) for training duties.

CONTENTS

Acknowledgements go to all those people who I have bored while writing this book. In particular my wife Gill, who spent countless hours reading the many versions that were produced. Also thanks go to Gerry Mead for his valuable comments on some of the bus related items. It just started out as a short story book of about twenty pages, but we kept finding more odd memories, old colleagues brought up others. Some readers may find they just have to comment on some of the bus related items, because they believe I'm not quite correct. Please remember the era in question was when London Country was struggling with a shortage of staff (good thing, otherwise I may not have been employed there) and also a shortage of the correct allocated vehicles, therefore lots happened that was not necessarily formally documented. Throughout it all, the company's objective was to run the best service possible with resources available, and generally they succeeded. Anyway my memory has done its best, and it was a long time ago. This book is not intended to be a history of vehicle workings; there are many excellent books written on that subject.

A JOB – ANY JOB

"So," said the voice at the end of the phone, "you want a job as a bus driver"? I hoped my reply didn't sound too pleading and that he wouldn't change his mind, seeing that he had just asked me what my last job was. My 13 years working in radio equipment design had suddenly come to an end when the firm decided to move from London to Leicester. Redundancy in itself isn't too much of a problem, unless you are about to sign up for a house mortgage, or you, wife and children are about to be evicted from your present rented dwelling because the owner has sold it.

According to my widowed aunt's bus inspector boyfriend there were vacancies at London Country's Leatherhead (LH) garage, and it would be a good quick source of income and give me the immediate employment I needed. "Come and see me on Tuesday," continued the Garage Traffic Superintendent. I could hardly wait, partly because like many boys I had always fancied driving a bus. On arriving at 8.30 prompt I was ushered into a small office, which was already busy with inspectors and the Engineering Manager arguing over an SM with persistent problems. When the row died down I was given some short arithmetic questions to answer and also told to write a short essay on what I thought made a good bus conductor, so I included such things as correct blind displays, helping old people onto the bus, generally being polite etc. Watching his face when he read it, I detected a smile in places, which at the time mystified me, but months later and following a bit of experience, it dawned on me the person I depicted in my make-believe was what he would have liked from his staff!

The arrival of a Driving Assessor prompted many questions about my driving experience, in particular had I ever driven a bus before or anything bigger than my Mini van? I didn't think a tractor pulling a lawnmower was relevant, so to both questions I replied "No." I was beginning to think I was doomed. I couldn't really tell him of the times of about twenty years previously, when a couple of us lads befriended a driver at the terminus of the 419, and that he often used to let us sit in the driver's seat and pretend we were driving the RF. At his departure time he actually let us start it up, and because we had expelled all the air in our make-believe driving, told us to rev it up with our foot on the operating pedal until the flag went up. He even let us select the starting gear. And it was the teaching of these two small operations that very soon came in useful.

Then as we walked out of the office I remembered one other short encounter with a London Bus. When I was working at Decca Radio and Television at Battersea, the company bought RTW 208, with the intention of converting it to a mobile showroom to go round to their dealers and show off the latest radiograms and records. The reason for 208, was that at that time Radio Luxembourg was the station one listened to for the latest pops, and that broadcast on 208 metres. The RTW was partially stripped – I acquired some of the seat cushions to fit in the rear of my Mini–van, but the project was never finished and one day the bus just disappeared from the site.

In the rear yard of LH garage was parked the trainer RT, where I was shown the controls of the bus; then with the Assessor at the wheel, off we went in the direction of Guildford, struggling up Hawks Hill and barely making it in 2nd gear. The bus was filled with bags of sand to simulate passengers. At the bus stop opposite Ridgeway we stopped, he got out and in a tongue I later found was quite normal, said "Up you get lad – make yourself comfortable."

In the past few days I had gone over all I could remember from my bus driver watching from years back, and on the day before, even went for a ride to view a driver in action. So with nerves all over the place, I selected 2nd gear, remembering from all those years ago being told to apply the foot brake before lifting the operating pedal, then pre-selected 3rd, used the mirrors both sides, indicated, released the hand brake, foot to the floor on the accelerator and off we crawled; God, aren't buses gutless I thought. After what seemed like a lifetime we gathered speed and 3rd was successfully obtained and later likewise 4th, both with no hassle. Even the downshift to 3rd to pass some road works proved successful with me remembering to rev up before I lifted the operating pedal.

At Woodlands Road I was directed into the bay used for terminating buses. To leave this bay and return to Leatherhead meant an almost full lock right turn into the main road from a slope. This I considered needed 1st gear. So I duly selected it, then pre-selected 2nd. However, pulling this heap around under these conditions took some effort, but I succeeded, and got it into 2nd without it leaping violently forward – I was beginning to relax just a little.

The journey back was uneventful until we approached the top of Hawks Hill. A bit steep I thought at 1 in 10 for top gear. The down change into 3rd was so well executed it even surprised me. After it the Assessor leant through into the cab and said, "You just beat me, I was just about to tell you to do that."

Soon we were stationary in the garage and I was bombarded with endless Highway Code questions, something I was reasonably confident with as I had recently taught my mother to drive, and it was still alive in my mind. He then asked again, "Are you sure you've never driven a bus before, you soon got the hang of it?" "Honest" I said, "no." What a compliment. Perhaps my recent driver watching came in useful after all. It was then back to the office with the news that I had the makings of a bus driver.

The visit to the medical man went without any problem and I was accepted; I had a job and I could get my mortgage.

THE TRAINING

Early morning on Monday 30th April 1973 saw me on my way to the Reigate (RG) training centre in my favourite front downstairs seat in an RMC – newly introduced on the 406 – and it was on that journey that I became conscious of the peculiarities of the direct change gear system. The gearbox appeared to hang on to 2nd gear although the driver had put it in neutral, and because he had released the accelerator this caused the bus to "engine brake" until the gear released, and gave a double jerk to the ride. There must be a knack to get a better ride, I thought.

It had been many, many years since I had been into Reigate garage. During the mid-50s this was often my Sunday afternoon cycle ride, to view the collection of trams and trolleybuses stored there, before they found a home at The Museum of British Transport at Clapham. And when I asked an oldish man in the little office where the training room was, I am sure he was the same one who allowed us to look at the old vehicles those many years previously. "What you again?" he would say, "OK, but remember no climbing." They were now long gone, their place taken by a row of brand new Nationals soon to replace RFs on Green Line 711. After the first of the many visits to the gents that morning (why is it you have to go more often when it's cold and you are a bit apprehensive?) I knocked and entered the training room. After some basic introductions, my first instruction was in how a fluid flywheel worked, and this was probably because I showed some interest in the model of it. This was followed by a general talk on passenger safety, plus information on what to expect during the training sessions.

On day two I am assigned to instructor Sid and, along with two other new entrants, am taken to the bus, the same one I was assessed on, which from memory was RT 2777. After a quick show round it, off we went towards Gatwick with Sid at the wheel. At the top of Cockshot Hill he decided to turn right and only just made it in front of an approaching car. "Bit close," he murmured. "This old girl's a bit slow loaded like this, so don't forget it." He continued shouting various messages until finally stopping near Gatwick, where he selected one of the others for a first go. "Where shall we go to today?" he enquired. The one in the seat, a bit of a comic said "Brighton." "Right" said Sid, "you're pointing that way, get going." "And what's your name again?" "Mike" came the answer. It was a good choice as the road is reasonably straight and wide; good to get acquainted with the vehicle.

On arrival at Brighton we took refreshments in the bus station, after which, with the other trainee (Brian) then at the wheel, we were forced to go via the other end of the prom for a cursory glance at the topless bathers from the top deck. Both drivers had made many hashes along the way resulting in derisory remarks from Sid about their parents' marital status.

Will I get a turn today, I wondered? Not, it turned out, until we got off the straight dual carriageway on to the twisty, single roads past Crawley. It's not fair, I thought; they got the easy bits; what mess can I make, considering how they faired on the wider roads? Not only that, but now it was literally falling down with rain and the cab was steamed up like a sauna; this is not to be my day. I also detected that Sid seemed to be getting progressively rattier. Once in the seat with Sid leaning through the window space from the saloon, the two rings of the bell woke me up; why so loud? Off we go; 2nd, 3rd, top, down the slight gradient, along the straight, past Sidlow Bridge, round the curve, keep going, see the red lights, good they've just gone to green, just keep going, should be okay, a hill ahead, let's try a down change, success it worked, stay in that I thought as the hill falls away, little bit of engine braking needed and we're going to turn right in a moment. However this meant going into 2nd gear on the move before entering the turn. My God is with me; that worked as well; into the garage slowly we went. "Think you can park it between those two?" said Sid "without scratching them" – "I'll try" I murmured – pause – "backwards of course" he then adds, "then it's ready for tomorrow." Judging by how he got with the others, I reckon he's looking for something to shout at me about, I thought. Oh well, straight ahead, bit of right lock, bags of left, stop, hand brake, select reverse using two hands, and now creep back on tickover into the gap. "Use the nearside mirror and lean out of the door, and use the other bus as a guide line," shouts Sid. "Not bad" followed, then, "you can switch it off now Rod, and you can remove your cycle clips, they weren't needed after all." I felt quite relieved and even quite pleased with my effort after that.

Day three was taken up mainly in making us look beautiful. The uniform store turned out to be a pretty run-down building in a field shared with some sorry looking buses next to Chelsham garage. I don't know who gave the patterns for the uniform; whatever size I tried nothing seemed to fit. The one advantage was that the canteen also shared the same building. Chelsham is situated in a high and bleak part of the Surrey/Kent border where cold is even colder. There were rumours that during these excessive cold spells the RTs were started up at regular intervals during the night just to keep them warmer. A slight detour on the return journey, to deliver some uniforms, showed that Chelsham was not the only location where the garage and canteen were separated by a short walk; East Grinstead canteen was in an establishment that resembled an old house.

Day four started in a similar way with Brian going first, but with the announcement that we're going to pick up some paperwork at the Traffic Office near Pentonville Road. Near Vauxhall, we stopped for all to have a leak, then "Up you get Rod"; why me for the hard bit again? By the Houses of Parliament my worst fears were supported, "Straight on up Whitehall" he bellowed, knowing at the end lingered Trafalgar Square, that mass of roads where traffic mingled at such alarming rates.

Past the Whitehall theatre, where I had once worked, the lights were just changing to green, so with a good drop to 3rd and with Sid's hot breath down my collar asking "Do you know which way to Charing Cross Road?", it was all systems go. Many times I had done the manoeuvre in a car, but in a sluggish old bus with no power to get out of trouble? The knack was of course to indicate your intentions, keep going and mingle; and that's what I did. "No problem," Sid said afterwards, obviously sensing my nerves. It may seem strange now why one has these feelings, but at the time it was all quite a harrowing experience and anyone who says otherwise probably is trying to kid themselves. It never should be forgotten how large, cumbersome and potentially lethal are these beasts.

I did receive my share of Sid's voice on several occasions that day. "Stop driving it like a piano," he would say. Pianos apparently have two pedals and you use one foot between them. I either had my foot on the accelerator or the brake. "Get your eyes up, look ahead more, buses coast a long way." The trip back to Reigate was uneventful except for Brian not knowing his left from right. As we went straight past the road Sid had told him to turn into, Sid said to me whilst looking down that road, "You know Rod, I was bloody sure we were going to go down there."

Day five was also highlighted by Brian's actions. By now he was beginning to get very confident, but in taking a sharp right turn too fast in a very narrow lane near Tinsley Green, we didn't make the corner and instead went through a wire mesh fence. The only damage was a small dent on the wing, and it did take some of his cockiness away.

Day six was spent with me alone in the training centre with Les, learning the ins and outs of Gibson, Setright and Almex ticket machines and the rather illogical fares system. Children were charged at the adult rate before 9.30 and between the hours of 16.00 to 19.00, and also at these times the adult fare was raised by 1p. Neither condition applied in the GLC area.

How to deal with all the various forms that would be encountered was an exercise on its own. When a conductor or One Man Operation (OMO) driver reported for duty he/she quoted the duty number, and was given a box. In this box were many things, including a ticket machine and various forms. Probably the most important form was the waybill, and on this was recorded all the transactions relating to one particular ticket machine, from the moment of issue to when returned to the garage depot office.

Before leaving the Conductor's Room you carefully checked that all entries on the waybill agreed with the ticket machine readings. Otherwise you would be liable (in monetary terms) for any discrepancies.

There was a second waybill, and this related to the emergency tickets, which one used if the main ticket machine failed. This was sealed in a polythene bag, which also housed the emergency tickets. These had pre-printed fares on them, and were of similar form to the old thick paper ones. Like those, they had fare stage numbers printed down each side back and front, and one was supposed to punch a hole or put a tear at the fare stage where the passenger boarded. If the bag was returned intact, it was not necessary to fill in the emergency waybill.

The style of the main waybill varied depending on what ticket machine it was attached to. A crew conductor would be issued a Gibson machine, and this waybill had two days' worth of entries, and included an entry for each denomination. This was because the Gibson machine was capable of issuing fourteen different values of tickets, and had a read-out for each one. So at the end of each day, it was necessary to write down the final numbers for each, and then work out how many of each were sold, then do a grand total of that quantity times the actual price of each. And that was the money you paid in. The machine also had a read-out for ticket numbers and these were noted on the waybill at the end of each journey. Some routes required entries for what was known as "Point entries", and these were points along the journey where ticket numbers were recorded. These were used for evaluating passenger loadings.

For OMO, Leatherhead used Almex II machines and these gave readings for halfpennies, one penny, and ten pence, so the actual total analysis was quite easy. For the ten pence grand total, you multiplied the actual ticket numbers sold, by ten, the one penny by one, and generally you didn't sell any halfpennies. There was also a display for the actual ticket numbers. These machines could only issue tickets up to a maximum of 99 pence. Anything over that needed a multiple issue, but that only occurred on some return fares.

On all tickets, apart from the fare, was printed the boarding fare stage number, the ticket number, the ticket machine number and ticket class code, and that varied between ticket machine types.

From this it was possible to tell where a ticket was valid to. That was assuming that the correct data was set by the person who issued it. There were many occasions when passengers offered a return ticket (correct code AR) that was coded as a single (AS). A quick question of where did they board and a comparison with the price paid usually sorted that out.

Although I was trained on 'Setrights' I never used one in service, so I cannot comment on that machine. We had to know about the Setright printed codes, because other garages that shared our routes sometimes still used them

All moneys paid in had to be correctly bagged in separate denominations, and for this, a selection of different denomination money bags would be included in the box.

The provision of adequate float was down to the conductor. I personally always had quite a large float, as it made life easier, particularly early in the morning, when no one seemed to have "anything small". Some conductors would not change big notes, and referred passengers to a local newsagent to get "something smaller". I know of several occasions where a passenger asked for a 10p fare and tendered a £5 note for it, and for the change, the conductor found a bag containing £5 worth of 10p coins he had previously bagged, removed one of the 10p and handed the rest to the passenger as change. The passenger might have said, "Sorry I have nothing smaller," whereupon the conductor would say, "well you'll have no trouble next time." Happy Days!

Another item in the box was the duty card. This listed all the vehicle running numbers, times, meal breaks and places of changeover relating to that particular duty.

If you are the first driver to take out a particular vehicle, then you will also be given the vehicle card. On that will be stated the running number from the originating garage – for example LH 52. That card stayed with the vehicle all day, and was removed by the last driver who handed it back to the depot office and also signed the vehicle defect sheet, which was also in the conductor's room.

Several other forms in the box included an unpaid fare form and sometimes an up to date list of persons who have given false details on numerous occasions on unpaid fare forms. It was normal to accept for travel persons who had insufficient funds, on the proviso that they sent the unpaid amount to the company. Some abused that privilege.

Two forms stayed with the bus. One was known as an 'auxiliary waybill', and was used when a particular conductor was not doing the complete journey of that bus. It recorded their start and finish ticket numbers relating to that last journey. This form was what you – as the conductor who had taken over – handed to an inspector (or 'Jumper' as they were known), along with your own start numbers.

Unpaid/Excess fare sheet. This was used to take a passenger's details when they were unable to furnish the required fare. The same form could also be used by the driver to claim a refund for a ticket issued in error. For this all the relevant particulars had to be filled in, and it meant asking the passenger for some assistance; some were loath to do.

UNPAID FARE
UNPAID EXCESS FARE   B   74574   B   74574
TICKET ISSUED IN ERROR
(Delete wording not applicable)

Garage_____197___
Conductor's name (BLOCK letters)_____
Badge No_____ Route No_____ Duty No_____ Machine No_____
                                               State whether verified
*Passenger's name_____ If so, how
(BLOCK letters)
*Address_____
(BLOCK letters)
Boarded at_____ Time_____hr.

Alighted at_____
           Fare due to   State whether
Ticket No_____ London Country_____ credit required_____
If another ticket issued state value_____
If punched or issued in error } (a) Number_____ (b) Value_____
attach ticket to this form and state }
      CONDUCTOR'S REPORT (where necessary) see over
*Credit to Conductors will not be allowed unless this information is given
        TO BE HANDED IN TO THE GARAGE OFFICE

LONDON COUNTRY BUS SERVICES LTD
BELL STREET, REIGATE, SURREY

In consideration of London Country Bus Services Ltd having permitted you to travel on a Public Service vehicle when not in a position to pay the appropriate fare in accordance with the Public Service Vehicle Regulations you are required to forward by post to the Traffic Manager, Bell Street, Reigate, Surrey, or pay at any London Country garage within seven days the sum of

being the fare due

Please present or forward this form, showing your name and address on the reverse, at time of payment.

Date of travel_____ 197___
TO BE HANDED TO THE PASSENGER

The other form that remained on the bus was the 'Log Sheet' and this was filled in at the end of each journey. It had places for entering the timetabled arrival and departure times and two more columns for the actual times both early and late. But you never admitted to being early.

If you were running late, overtime could be claimed for partial loss of meal-break or for over-running your end of duty sign-off time. And in those circumstances you made sure that the late figure you entered on the log sheet agreed with the overtime docket you presented to the office.

On the other side of the log sheet, the 'staff details' section listed persons responsible for that bus at a particular time. It required a record of the driver's and conductor's names and their badge numbers and duty number.

It must be remembered that following successful training, conductors were also issued with a badge. It was of similar style to a driver's, but coloured green instead of red, and like the driver's one, it had to be displayed. OMO drivers were supposed to display both Driver and Conductor badges. In practice only a few did.

There were many rules concerning the carriage of passengers, and these had been recorded onto a tape. For this Les produced a rather ancient looking battered tape machine and said it would sound poor, but we should get the gist of it. He was right; it produced a very muffled sound. Two minutes was all I could stand of this when I said, "Would you like that fixed?"

"You can try" said a voice from the back room office, "others have and failed." Inspection of the machine showed that the tape head adjusting screws were severely chewed up – someone had been playing, and lots of times. Anyway after a quick clean of the heads with a spat-on handkerchief and then adjusting the head alignment to the tape on it, the result was quite surprising, to which 'the voice' suggested that I go down in the garage and help get some of the new Nationals sorted out and on the road. The 'voice' belonged to a Mr Perfect who introduced himself as perfect in name only. Robin Perfect was in charge of training and Les was his number one. Every so often Les would drag me out into the smelly garage for yet another quick look at something like blind displays or how to stop an engine in emergency. It quickly became apparent what he really wanted was a smoke. Smoking wasn't allowed in the training room. Many years earlier this Les had been a driver at Reigate, and he told me of an occasion when, during one of the many thick fogs we used to have, he got lost and nearly drove a Q-type through a pond near Earlswood!

Life as a trainee settled to a regular routine of leaving Reigate about 8.30. The instructor had been changed to Ray, a so-called temporary man as his real job was a driver on the coaches. These temporary men were drivers who were considered to have the necessary skills and were trained to act as instructors when full time instructors were overloaded with work. Ray had quite a humour and he seemed to have a love of the roads around Willesden and the back of King's Cross, where we practised most of our reversing.

It was whilst on one of the upward trips we were shown what the driving test route would most probably be. The starting point was outside the BBC Theatre on Shepherd's Bush Green, then turn left into Uxbridge Road. Then the directions from the examiner would probably immediately be take the next "available" right turn, which actually is about the third, as the first one is a Cul de Sac and the second a No Entry. This proved to be a good tip from Ray.

One morning we were informed that it was driving assessment day with our Mr Perfect accompanying Ray. Les came along for the ride (and a smoke upstairs) and said in his usual sarcastic way, "Don't worry too much about Perfect; his own driving is none too clever, and at heart all he really wants is you all to succeed." There were a few comments about changing down going up hill. Despite repeated tellings, Brian still insisted on revving up with his foot down on the operating pedal and when the revs had died down taking it off. The result was a jolt as the bus slowed down because the revs were wrong for the gear selected at that particular road speed. Pre-selection is built around the principle of thinking which gear you may need next and when going up a hill, a lower gear fits the bill. This was the method taught by London Transport.

The next day, due to a shortage of drivers Ray was put back driving a 727 and another instructor took us out for a few days. I believe his name was John. It is interesting how different instructors have different views. We were now on our third, and John's view on what gear to pre-select approaching a roundabout differed from Ray's. Ray said 2nd, John said 3rd. But they both agreed on the general problem of 'down pre-selection', in that if you didn't use it you needed to remember to 'up pre-select' later. If you didn't, you had a good chance of standing the bus on its nose. (This is because you may be going faster and would go down a gear instead of up). I tended not to pre-select anything until I was absolutely sure of what I wanted next. Unfortunately, on the test you had to drive to 'The Book'.

The good thing about today was the weather; beautiful sun, acceptably warm, but not too much. John was enjoying this, as it brought out the short skirts along the Kings Road where we were just approaching. The bad thing was Mick's driving. Even he was apparently having trouble with down changes, and these were at slow speed in traffic. Brian claimed the bus was at fault. "Rubbish" replied John, "you're both just useless, have you not learnt anything during your training?" I kept quiet. "Pull over, I will demonstrate." Up jumped John and showed off the wonders of a good down change. "Have you lot got it?" he chanted; no reply from us – he tried again. Still no response. On looking round, he soon saw why; we were more interested in looking at the action walking on the pavement than John's.

Brian and Mike, hearing of John's love of the Kings Road and what it offered with sunny weather at that time of day, decided we should get a share of the action and for us to fully concentrate on what was on offer meant that

John would have to drive; however he wouldn't be consulted. Luckily he took it in good faith when he realised the joke, but we had a hard time for the rest of the day and had to buy him tea.

Probably the best highlight of our tours of west London was a visit to Chiswick. This we were told about the day before as it was important that we all had clean shoes, correct tie, good shirt and so on. We were representing London Country and had to look the part; no scruffiness here. This was a very important occasion and we were all quite excited by it. We even stayed late the night before and gave the old bus a wash over.

Approaching the main security at Chiswick, apprehension filled us; would we be allowed in with our 'foreign' vehicle, as some previously had been refused entry. Luck was with us, as we were waved through and parked along the road adjacent to the skid patch.

After a quick snack in their huge canteen, Ray left us, and on returning called us over to where we were introduced to a skid instructor. Ray had been trained at Chiswick, and found an old colleague who did his bit and got us a ride on the skid RT with some unofficial instruction – unfortunately not with us at the wheel; but what an experience.

We all went home on a high that day, until we arrived back at Reigate, where in the training office Mike and I were told we had been considered as candidates for the test in two days time. Brian needed more pushing, and in fact even after four chances, never passed and was later dismissed. Normally one was given two chances, in exceptional cases three, but somehow Brian managed to get four. We believed he was given that extra chance because he had had the same examiner for two consecutive tests.

AN 26 from the first batch of two door examples sporting its as delivered colours, waits at the layover stop at Effingham 'Sir Douglas Haig' in May 1976. *Ian Pringle*

THAT DREADED DAY

Those two days passed too quickly. Both Mike and I said we didn't sleep too well the night before, but the sun was shining on 23rd May 1973 as we set off bright and early for Shepherd's Bush.

Mike chose to go first, I was banished to the upper quarters. Sure enough we turned left into Uxbridge Road and took that first "available" right turn. At the end it was left on to the busy fast moving A40. Then after the lights and up the hill we turned left and sharp right toward Acton. It was on this sharp right that Mike scraped the curb; poor Mike I thought, he knows that's a probable failure point. Then he sat for a long time in stationary traffic on the North Circular in second gear, I kept saying out loud, "Put it in neutral Mike," but of course he couldn't hear me. He was failed on these two points.

Eventually we got to Stonebridge garage and it was my turn; out towards Hanger Lane and towards Chiswick High Road. The lights were red at the crossroads by Turnham Green. Just as I applied the handbrake I noticed a van parked the other side of the lights, which I should have seen earlier as it was blocking my lane. Too late now, make the best of it. Mirror, indicate, hand out of window to reinforce my intentions – and go.

The next problem was horrendous – when on test anyway, and my actions were not ones I'd recommend on a test unless you definitely want to fail. There is a very sharp corner at the end approaching Hammersmith in the one-way bit, and right on that corner on the opposite side a lorry had broken down blocking most of the road. Although cars were getting past, there was no way a bus would. At my turn I just stopped, and sensing how in a few minutes Hammersmith would become locked up, I turned around and gave notice to the examiner of my intentions, which was to mount the pavement slightly as I had seen a bus in front do. I made an overdone example of looking for overhanging objects on the pavement and for pedestrians, then proceeded very slowly, particularly when bumping down again. The test was to terminate within Shepherd's Bush garage, and I was directed to stop for him to view a suitable parking slot, "Over there" he pointed, "stick it in backwards" between those two. Done that before I thought, on my first day, but a lot tighter this one. As before take it slowly, don't show off, just get it right. "OK that'll do, switch off but stay there until I call." Poor Mike was having his Highway Code questions and notice of his failure.

My turn to be grilled now – lots of Highway Code questions, then I was asked how did I think I did? I told of the mistake at the traffic lights by being in the wrong lane; his reply was I should have seen it and straddled both lanes. Next came the pavement bit. To my amazement he didn't seem too bothered, and was content that I knew and commented on what I was about to do and took the proper precautions before executing the manoeuvre. His only comment to Ray was that this lad knew his mistakes. That I did, only too well – I passed!

LEARNING ALL THE TYPES

It was a requirement to be 'type trained' on all the types you were expected to drive and my first type was an RF. For this we borrowed a Green Line one. Could this bus shift, and so light compared to our old loaded RT. Only half a day was given and we made ourselves useful by taking some paperwork up to the Pentonville Road Traffic Office. Afterwards we got diverted on foot to the nearby Chapel Market where some cheap shirts were on offer. Returning home Ray accused me of driving too slow, "Get a move on Lad". OK, if that's what he wants. The 50 mph along a short bit of the A3 was quite a dream in an RF, and he was happy as well.

Type training continued with the SM, which although fitted with a semi-automatic gear system had a position on the gear selector switch with 'A' against it. The only indication that it was not fully automatic (like the Central area ones) was a small sticker above the windscreen. The AN followed, which was described as "a sluggish heap but feels like an arm-chair". The last type train was on an RMC following the 408 route from Leatherhead to Guildford and back with many stops on the return leg. The RMC, like the SM and AN, is fitted with a semi-automatic gearbox and to get a decent gear change relies solely on the driver's timing co-ordination between operating the accelerator pedal and the gear lever. Les, who didn't like 'power up-changes' was insistent that I mastered the 2nd–3rd gear change without a double lurch. My reminiscing to him of my first time riding on one and the comments I made about the poor performance by that driver brought that on.

An unofficial type train was the opportunity to drive a brand new National. My initial training buddy who had now been successful in his test was going to Dorking, where Nationals were being introduced, so he needed type training. On the morning in question I was at Reigate about to travel to Leatherhead to start route learning and over the regulation canteen tea they offered to go via Leatherhead and give me a lift. Approaching Dorking I asked "Can I have a go?". The answer "Why not" surprised me. I drove from Dorking North Station via the narrow bit past Mickleham Church, to Bridge Street, Leatherhead. Anyway, what was very unusual was that the unofficial bit of type training was recorded as "acceptable for service" on my staff record.

What did strike me as an oversight was that at LH we were not type trained on MB buses, which were quite different in the door controls and were longer than SMs. These, Leatherhead drivers would drive on the second half of Sunday duty 203 on the 406 as RG 32. Driving buses from RG and GF that shared the same routes was quite normal, but for some reason Addlestone (WY) was exempt from that arrangement. In fact some weekday 406 RG buses stabled overnight at LH and emerged as an LH allocation the next day. The next night they went back to RG. In reverse some 406 LH buses slept overnight at RG.

RT 2836 on route 71 and a couple of two door ANs on the forecourt of Leatherhead garage. The 71 was one way we used to get to Kingston to take up duties from there. For me to use the 71, I was issued with a 'staff on duty pass' as my LCBS pass didn't cover me on LT routes. Some of the 'old timers' had passes that allowed them to use Green Line route 714 which stopped outside the Bull pub in Leatherhead town. Some little time later route 71 was converted to single deck OPO, was renumbered 265 and was allocated the BL class.

DRIVING TIPS

With driver training, the idea was to get the driver and vehicle to become one and up to a point it was repetition that was practised to achieve this. Methods and procedures were drummed into you so they became an automatic operation – such things as, when you stopped at a bus stop or for more than a few seconds you always applied the handbrake, and if for longer than about two minutes, you also selected neutral.

When you started the engine of a pre-selector, you always did it with the operating pedal depressed irrespective of whether the flag was up or down; this reminded you to do it when the flag was down. Never did you know if the bus had been left in a gear or neutral. It is not possible to select neutral or another gear with little or no air, so you could therefore start it in gear, and if you then revved it to get the air up with the operating pedal up, you had a good chance of the bus moving at dramatic knots when the air pressure increased and the gears bit! Depressing the operating pedal effectively disengaged all the gears

A similar warning applied to semi-automatics. They couldn't be started with the gear lever in a gear position. Once started, a gear could immediately be requested, but would not be available if the air was low. The natural instinct was to rev the engine to get the air up quickly, but you had to remember that if the gear lever was left in a gear you would get that gear when the air rose. In later years there was a nasty accident in a garage because of this, as the driver had also released the handbrake.

RT 4117 the one who's engine was often very difficult to stop. On one occasion I couldn't turn it off at Redhill, so on the return past Reigate garage I decided to request assistance, but of course when the fitter tried it stopped immediately. He was nice about it though and suggested that it probably stopped OK then because it had been idling for some while.
Roy Hobbs

Some engines of RTs (4117 in particular) and RFs were difficult to stop, and one method suggested was to leave the bus in gear, which caused a slower tickover, and select neutral after it had stopped. Another method used to stop an obstinate engine on a pre-selector was to rev up the engine then drop the operating pedal with top selected. It generally worked, but it could be dangerous. I saw a near accident in the garage when two buses were closely parked with one fitter standing between them and another one in the bus trying to stall it. When the fitter in the bus dropped the operating pedal it leapt forward and sandwiched the other fitter between the two buses. Luckily he was thin.

Of all the classes, RTs probably had the best visibility, and narrow gaps could be gauged very accurately. And to help, the small nearside mirrors had somehow been adjusted to show the side of the bus with a small glimpse of the rear nearside wheels – very useful except in one way streets where one had to lean sideways slightly to view traffic, but still the best option. With all types, when pulling away from a stop, you always looked in the nearside mirror to check for passengers who may be trying to board when you were moving, even on a doored bus. Likewise you looked down on your right side for cyclists or pedestrians that you may have missed in your right mirror, but never, never moved forward with your eyes not looking ahead.

RMC 1464 departing from Reigate Red Cross on the long journey to Kingston. *Roy Hobbs*

RMCs were of course six inches wider than RTs, but had bigger mirrors. There was a story of one of the 'Old Timers' who when going up Ewell High Street one day in an RMC on the 406 forgot about this extra width and managed to clout several car mirrors without doing any other damage to the car bodywork.

SMs, MBs and to a lesser degree ANs, had very long overhangs both back and front. This meant that a different driving technique to RTs and RMCs was required. One could go up to within about four feet of a bus in front at a bus stop, and by turning to full steering lock be able to clear that bus. However by doing this, the rear would swing over the pavement and could come in contact with items close by. A circumstance where this can happen is in a row of parked cars in a narrow street, where it may mean 'snaking' to get through the obstacles.

An example of this happened at the crossroads at the top of Surbiton Hill, where the road divided into two traffic lanes, one for straight on and left, the other for right turn only. The 418 turned right there, and one night an SM was doing this sharp manoeuvre when a car shot up the inside, and when the bus swung round the rear overhang caught the car – no it wasn't me driving! Really the bus driver should have spotted the car, as we were instructed to use the nearside mirror to check under such circumstances.

In general when trying to pass obstacles that are blocking your side, don't go right up to them, but hang back with your right indicator on. It makes you more obvious to oncoming traffic and because you are further back from the obstacle you don't have to snake about so much. There was a stout warning about care being needed when going through narrow gaps where oncoming traffic was concerned; you may be quite happy about the manoeuvre but some car drivers may become frightened at the prospect of a big bus that close and lose their nerve and a collision could occur.

One day, whilst travelling on the A3, we witnessed a side-swipe directly in front of us on the three lane section, where a car in the outside lane decided to go to the middle lane to allow someone to pass, but didn't indicate this move. At the same time a car in the inside lane decided to go to the middle lane to overtake someone. He had indicated, but it was one of those indicate and immediately go moves. Ray often said to be careful of Volvo cars, "many don't have working indicators and of the remainder, their drivers think it below their dignity to use them".

When braking, try to do it gently and just before coming to a halt, lift your foot slightly off the pedal to reduce the braking effect; this allows the suspension to catch up and stops that final lurch so much a characteristic of some drivers. This doesn't mean you have to drive slowly, you just need to, as you were told, "get your eyes up, look far ahead, and plan your manoeuvres." You can watch the effect on passengers on a bus where the driver drives roughly and erratically. Passengers stay sat down until the vehicle has stopped, which increases the dwell times at stops, and loses any time gained by tearing about.

Skid patch training had unfortunately been lost when London Transport Country Buses became London Country Bus Services, and what replaced it was just emergency stop training. This consisted of the instructor banging on the handrail behind the driver with the expected response being that the bus stopped very quickly, preferably without skidding, and the brakes being released just before you were stationary to remove that jerk mentioned earlier. Don't forget the handbrake when you've stopped – and as always with the lever type handbrake, don't whatever you do drag the handbrake over the ratchet; always squeeze up the release lever.

Being country routes with lots of overhanging trees, one was made aware of such, with the instruction to report any bad ones so they could be attended to. And with double deckers you also had to be careful of any upright obstacles close to the roads with steep cambers, and of course low bridges.

Unless very heavily loaded or on a steep hill, the preferred starting gear on a four speed bus was 2nd. There were some drivers who were so automatic in their driving methods that even under those conditions allowed the vehicle to plod away from a stop in 2nd. Either that or they couldn't get a decent 1st to 2nd change so gave up the idea. You were dissuaded from using first on the flat because it was considered that the sharp acceleration may be uncomfortable to passengers, particularly as some may still be standing and finding their seats. The method of changing down gears depended on the circumstances and transmission type.

Going up hill with a pre-selector, first ensure you have selected the lower gear, then keeping your foot down on the accelerator, depress and then almost immediately release the operating pedal. The length of time you kept it depressed allowed the engine to speed up for the lower gear and it was this depression time that one judged for a good smooth gear change. If you merely wanted a lower gear on the flat or when descending a hill, first ensure the speed is not too fast for the lower gear, then that you have selected the lower gear, depress the operating pedal and at the same time rev up the engine and quickly release the operating pedal. The idea being to match the speed of the engine for that new lower gear to your road speed. Except at very very low speeds, you never just let the pedal up without this rev matching. Apparently if you did there was a chance of breaking the bands in the gearbox. And on no account did you ever try to use the operating pedal like a conventional clutch.

Driving both pre-selectors and direct-selectors, confusion between them was easy if not paying attention. With direct selection as on RMC, AN and SM the technique taught varied slightly between the RMC and others, mainly because the RMC did not release the gears instantly, meaning that although you had selected neutral it was some two or three seconds later when that happened. This often became apparent when reversing; if you selected forward quickly the bus wouldn't move because reverse was still mechanically engaged. In the mornings when cold, some RMCs wouldn't give 1st. I nearly came unstuck on the hill at the traffic lights in Leatherhead High Street – releasing the handbrake I had no gears and the bus rolled backwards. (I know I should have let the bus pull me off the handbrake, but it was 5.40 in the morning).

Generally when changing up, one moved the gear lever to neutral, released the accelerator, waited till the engine revs had dropped sufficiently for the new higher gear, then selected it and re-applied the accelerator.

With RMCs, to allow for the slow gear drop out on 2nd–3rd, and to a lesser degree also 1st–2nd, you kept your foot on the accelerator for about two seconds after moving the gear to neutral. If you didn't, because you had no throttle, engine braking occurred. You could of course keep your foot down and do 'power-up changes', and on 3rd–4th changes this was quite acceptable, but on 1st–2nd and 2nd–3rd at high revs, a nasty jolt often resulted.

It was strange to note that we were not taught that method, but it was the one suggested in the driver manual issued by London Country for RMCs. Later in life when London Transport took back the RCLs, which had exactly the same transmission system, their driver manual preferred the pause in neutral method. This didn't replicate what happened on their RMs which had fully automatic transmission, where the gears changed with power on.

As is well known, the quality of change varied from bus to bus, as it relied very much on how the system had been set up, what the air pressure had been set to and whether the correct restrictors were fitted to the individual gears, and of course the condition of the brake bands. Many drivers premeditated the change and lifted their foot slightly to reduce the bite. The gear change points were originally set to give a combination of good fuel economy plus allow reasonable headway. During the fuel crisis of 1973 the up change points were lowered in the belief it would reduce fuel usage, but the result was the reverse because many drivers found the buses too slow and therefore used the manual over-ride facility.

With many RMCs I found that even on a flat road 1st was needed when loaded. I usually got the bus just moving and quickly changed to 2nd. If the revs were low, you could change with your foot still on the gas and get a good change without a 'snatch'. I put down the need to use 1st to the high speed differential fitted, plus the fact that they were designed for Green Line use and initially had their engine output set for that use. Certainly when they first arrived directly off Green Line they had more go in them; apparently they were later 'de-rated' for bus use to save fuel. I doubt if in practice this was the result, because it certainly made the engine do more work. It was at one time possible to get up most of Ashley Road hill from Epsom Town to The Downs in top gear, only needing 3rd at the very top, but following the de-rating you were sometimes struggling in 2nd. To change down going up hill you kept your foot on the gas and just moved the gear lever through to the next gear. The theory was that the time through neutral gave the engine time to speed up for the lower gear.

To get a good change needed practice, particularly if you were going across the gate i.e. 3rd–2nd, and of course all vehicles varied. On the flat or when about to descend a steep hill and you wanted a lower gear, if necessary you first reduced your road speed, then moved the lever to neutral, revved up enough to match the engine for the proposed gear at that road speed and quickly moved the gear lever to the lower gear. Again, because of gear hang on, it was sometimes better to move the lever to neutral for a second or two before the revving up. You never changed down without matching the engine revs to the road speed.

When approaching blind obstacles, sharp corners etc and coasting, one should not assume that the way will be clear and hover over the accelerator. Instead you should cover the brake, as the extra second needed for the foot to change position could make all the difference to your stopping distance. The stopping position at bus stops was very important, not only in the difference between front entrance and rear entrance vehicles, but also the stopping angle. Never should you stop with your rear sticking out, as the rear of the bus could obscure your view of oncoming traffic. If the stop was on a left hand curve, one trick we were given was to look in the nearside mirror to see past the bus to view the traffic.

When doing crew work, you soon noticed the difference between conductors, and this generally showed up in the dwell time at stops. A good conductor would 'hurry up' the passengers; just half a minute wasted at a stop could be difficult to recover, even with slick driving.

A good driver would watch the progress of passengers in the nearside mirror, and as the last was about to board, would view the traffic conditions with the offside one and begin to plan the pull-away tactics.

One of our RMCs, 1490, had been painted white and advertised London and Manchester Assurance, which really threw some passengers as all-over advertising on buses was in its infancy, and they didn't recognise it as a service bus. So you had to be ready for being hailed at the last moment if you had that bus.

FARES PLEASE

Looking back, to me the most boring bit of training was the week acting as a conductor on a crew bus, alongside a fully fledged man from my parent garage, Leatherhead. This is also the first time you have a feel of what is in store from the public – "fiddling so-and-sos" so Charlie the conductor instructor would warn me.

"Keep an eye on that fancy tart in the short skirt and tight top," he said the first morning on the way into Kingston on a 406. That, I was already doing but for a different reason. "She over-rides, she only pays to the Apple Market, but goes on to the Station." Sure enough she tried, but Eagle eyes (not me thankfully) caught her and she paid up.

It was during my time learning conducting and suffering several drivers that I realised how rough some were, and smoothness wasn't directly related to top speed either. The conductor definitely appreciated a better ride, as it made hanging on whilst giving a fare easier, particularly on RMCs as they had no vertical poles. Charlie was looking forward to me having a dose of school kids. With an RT we were to run dead to The Wells Estate, then a mix of 481 and 418 in service to Brettgrave, then as a 418 back to Epsom Station where we went into service as a 406 to Kingston. The school kids around Brettgrave were said to be "unruly"! But where were they? It was half term week for some schools, but the trip still ran. He seemed disappointed that I had got off lightly.

My only real mistake on conductor training was whilst on a 406 on a short working to Tadworth issuing a fare to someone to Redhill. I suppose I should have spotted that the distance from Tattenham Corner to Tadworth did not cost the 20p or so that I was asked for. Still Charlie wrote a message on the rear of the ticket asking the conductor of the next bus to accept the ticket. Whether he had had enough of me I don't know, but on the Saturday afternoon after the meal break in Reigate he told me to go home. "Try not to let anyone see you, we'll drop you off in Epsom."

Up pulled an RF whilst I was looking at the timetable when waiting in

Epsom for a bus back to Leatherhead. Funny I thought, nothing's due yet, and at this time of day they usually run on time.

The doors opened "Want a lift back?" came the cheery voice. "Thanks" I said, as I boarded this off-service bus (strictly illegal) driven by an inspector, and then was greeted by the Garage Traffic Superintendent (GTS), who seemed oblivious to the fact that I should still be on a 406 in the back streets of Redhill. Instead he questioned me on how was I doing, how was I finding things? What a splendid gentleman was this man John.

The following Monday my conductor training was cut short and instead I was given a list of routes that had to be learnt.

ROUTES AND BLINDS

One of the biggest problems for a new driver is to be aware of all the many odd turning points and short workings, apart that is from the normal official routes and school specials. Leatherhead certainly had its share of them all. I knew the locality around Epsom very well, Leatherhead reasonably, but Effingham and Guildford were another subject.

There was this once a day only, Leatherhead allocation on the 432 that meandered from Leatherhead to Effingham via the back lanes of Bookham. The driver I travelled with on the training run was at that time the Mayor of Epsom and Ewell, a Mr Tom Holland. What a mad humour; I think the next night he had an engagement with a speech filled with jokes and was trying them out on me.

There were colleagues from many backgrounds in similar circumstances to me, often looking for short-term employment to get past the problem of nothing available in their usual field, and using that as an excuse to realise a boyhood ambition, to drive a bus. Strangely this only applied to the male gender, there was no female distraction, but the passengers made up for that shortfall – it was a long hot summer.

One turn-round point that could be a little difficult was on the 416 and 422 at Boxhill, where the stand was a reverse move from the main road, which in itself was not very wide, and into the narrow space in front of the shop in Greenacres caravan site. And as there was no stop immediately before the stand, this could, theoretically mean an illegal operation, i.e. reversing with passengers on, who were of course often standing up ready to get off. I usually stopped on the main road a little way back for them to alight, and then put the nose just into the turning opposite, and reversed across the road, but before doing so made sure no one had parked a car in front of the shop, particularly at night as the street lighting there was very poor. Woodbridge terminus in Leatherhead on the 462 and 416 was a turning off the Kingston Road where one did a three-point turn at the triangle up a side road just before the estate. Another turn a few roads back was at Dilston Road. I never did that one, or learned it, and only became aware of it one day when perusing a timetable.

The turn in Cobham called 'Between Streets' on the 462 meant you turned right at the end of the parade of shops, found some place to layover for a while, then continued up and turned left on to the A3, then left again into Between Streets and back through Cobham.

There were several occasions where buses from route 406 were used on other routes, either before or after their main stint on the 406. It also had many journeys that ran short of the normal final destination.

A very odd 'short' we were told to do one night in the evening peak was Kingston to Stoneleigh by the Rembrandt Cinema, then round the round-about after the bridge and back to Kingston. Then a few nights later we were instructed by a 'Jumper' in Epsom to turn at Lower Kingswood – go down to The Mint Arms pub to where the red bus 80 turned, then return to Epsom; then go home. For the Epsom Downs shorts we did a U turn in the wide road outside the Grandstand. At Tolworth we used the small loop opposite The Red Lion pub where the trolleybus loop used to be, laying over on the wrong side of the road just as they did. Tattenham Corner shorts laid over at the 164A terminus stop, then did the loop via Tattenham Crescent and then turned right into the main road. There was an early evening 406 that returned from Tadworth to Leatherhead in service, but if you were on the Tadworth station turns that finished there and going back 'dead', and if there was no one on at the end of Kingswood Road, you didn't bother to go to the station but went back to Epsom via the 'Switchbacks' to Tattenham Corner.

One early morning 406 positioning journey started as a 408 from Effingham Woodlands Road and went via the 408 to Epsom Station, and there was an early evening 406 where the duty finished supporting the 462 by doing some 'rounders' between the Fetcham loop and Leatherhead. Throughout the daytime, the 462 was a single deck route and terminated by Leatherhead Station. Due to the low bridge on the approach road, the RT on the 462 terminated at the Kingston Road roundabout outside Downers hardware shop. And there was an odd schooldays afternoon start journey as a 481 which went from The Wells Estate to Epsom Brettgrave (on the 418 route) then back to Epsom Station where it changed to a 406. (I remember the day the 481 started with a CR with a duplicate on some journeys; it then went to GS then to RF.)

RTs still had all the route blinds left over from when they were the main class at Leatherhead, and included 406, 406A, 406E, 406F, 408, 416, 418, 418A, 462, 468, 470, 472 and 481. When on the 406/408 bits, the blind combination varied, depending on the conductor; some used 406 for the whole route from Effingham. Harry, a conductor I was paired with for a time, always set the 462s up correctly, mainly because it followed a short unofficial tea break, and also, as it started in the garage, eyes were upon you!

There was one late night 462 that continued through Cobham and Weybridge to Weybridge Hospital, in a dark narrow road just past the library.

The last 462 bus of the day went into the Rehabilitation College in Leatherhead. This was situated far beyond the station and when turning into the narrow drive from the unlit road one had to be aware of the ditch, or else you had the back wheels in there! How you got back from the college to the garage was a personal choice.

What generally threw you was the slight variation to what was usual on a route. For example the 416, usually Leatherhead to Boxhill, had a morning and a reciprocal afternoon journey that didn't turn right after Headley Common into Boxhill Road, but instead kept going on towards and through Walton on the Hill and terminated at Tadworth Station. The return route in Tadworth was via the Ashurst Road – Kingswood Road loop. One of the 406s terminating at Tadworth Station had a note on the time card which required the departure to be held for up to three minutes if the impending train arrival was delayed.

Some sections of the route to Boxhill were 'hail and ride', with the driver being able to stop at any safe point, but some passengers had some strange ideas on where safe points were.

On RT blinds there were three versions of intermediate displays that could be used for the 406. The full route from Kingston to Redhill included Kingswood, the shorter to Tadworth didn't, and the very short just said "Via Main Road". Some read "Via Epsom Road" and could be used for any route.

It was really the driver's job to change the front ultimate, but some conductors would do it for you, especially if there was a route change and you wanted some obscure one far down the blind, as it was quicker for them to do it upstairs when changing the others, than for the driver to look through the minute aperture in the cab and search for the backing writing that was often faded and impossible to read.

For a long time I had the theory that many passengers didn't read the blinds anyway. Arriving at Kingston from Redhill early one Saturday afternoon, Harry the conductor asked if we had had the correct ultimate, as several passengers had asked if we were going to Kingston. Waste of time I thought, we could put up anything, so on the return trip I did. The most obscure and also the cleanest, probably because it had only been used a few times when on the 408 or 470 some years back, was 'Sanderstead Fire Station'. At Redhill Harry reported that only two passengers on that very busy journey had questioned the display, which really proved the point. He also expressed disapproval of me, and said not to do it again.

Apart from Effingham on the 408 and Epsom for the 408 and 470, these two routes didn't have any official short turns. The 408 and 470, were run as a joint operation and there were many journeys where buses went into West Croydon as one route and emerged as another. I did notice 'Cheam' on some blinds and occasionally I turned them at Carshalton 'Windsor Castle' taking the old 654 trolley route to the end of Ruskin Road then left down to Carshalton High Street. For this turn I had to leave the ultimate blank.

RF 639 is seen about to enter LH garage in May 1974 after returning from its Wednesday and Sunday one single journey on route 472 from Netherne hospital. This vehicle is one of the non-refurbished variety and still had the single dip headlights fitted, which were not really acceptable on the unlit roads we traversed. On main beam both illuminated. *Colin Fradd*

One route where you would get a lot of help on the correct roads to take was the twice a week 472 limited stop service to Netherne Hospital, with passengers asking, "Now are you sure you know the way? The one last week got lost in Coulsdon." Probably why he got lost was because it was only done twice a year if you were on the rota, me being Mr Odd Job did it three Wednesdays in succession. This route only picked up people destined for the hospital, an establishment that specialised in treatment of people with a mental problem. In my opinion some of their visitors were a bit suspect also. One in particular had this horrible dribble problem and would persist in doing it over your ticket machine whilst waiting for her change.

The other event concerning the poor inhabitants of a mental hospital occurred on a 419 journey. I picked up a passenger at Horton Hospital and when terminating at Langley Vale noticed him still on the bus. On questioning him on where was he going, it became obvious that he was a patient, as he said he was going to London. So I said I would tell him when we got there, which as it happened was outside Horton Hospital on the return trip. Getting off he thanked me profusely.

But we've jumped a hell of a lot, so let's go back, nearly to the beginning.

The first class I drove in passenger service was the SM. Here is SM 105 on a weekday 418 working near West Ewell. *Ian Pringle*

OUT ON MY OWN

The next Wednesday after a morning route-learning trip from Tadworth to Esher on a 416, it was proposed that in the afternoon I did a refresher trip to Boxhill, but this was interrupted in the canteen by the news that the office manager wanted to see me downstairs. "I see you've done the Bookham bit of the 418, here's a ticket machine, there's an SM across the road running twenty minutes late, take it to Bookham and bring it back here in service, and don't hang about."

So started my service driving and it continued with the pattern as it had begun, to such an extent that I came to be known as 'Odd Job', as I was only on the crew rota list for a very short time. I was soon transferred back to the 'Instructions' list which actually I quite enjoyed. Life was never dull. I spent most of the time filling in for missing drivers, holiday cover, or with a bus filling in for for another one that was ages late.

The next day, my second out on my own, the inevitable happened; what every new and inexperienced driver dreads.

The road past the pond in Carshalton on the 408/470 is very narrow, with a high brick wall on one side and the pond on the other protected by just a few poles. The road also takes a double twist followed by a blind corner, so when returning from Croydon with the brick wall on your side you need to swing a bit wide so as not to scrape the wall. That's what I was doing, when at some terrific knots and much too fast for the road condition from the other direction came this large lorry. My AN stopped rather abruptly whence the lorry driver instructed me to reverse so he could pass. "Sorry," I said, "But buses are not allowed to reverse with passengers on, and there's no way they can get off with that wall in the way." He must have either believed me or seen the panic in my face, as eventually he reversed. This kind of happening just wasn't fair on my second day out!

The afternoon was taken up doing two covers with SMs on the Bookham end of the 418. The instructions for the second cover were, to take some passengers from outside Leatherhead garage on a very late running 418. But this time only go as far as there are passengers on your bus, after that turn it round somewhere and bring it back here – quick and dead.

After work I decided to visit mother who commented that a bus must have been seriously lost, as in that afternoon she had seen one creeping up Eastwick Road, the narrow road next to 'The Anchor' at Bookham. It was me mother, your crazy son, using it as a way between Lower Road and Guildford Road, and a quick way back to the garage. But I found that with parked cars the lower section of Eastwick Road is a bit narrow for a bus over eight feet wide.

T448, the 9T9 preserved by Cobham Bus Museum, at the old 419 stop in West Street Epsom. I had wanted to bring back the feeling of travelling up my old 419 route in a 9T9, and Bill Cottrell offered to do the driving. We were on route to another event. *Author*

A RETURN TO MY PAST

My first all-day proper cover job – two days after that first job with the SM – was on the first out 419 to Langley Vale. I was born in Langley Vale, and spent the first twenty years of my life there, and for about twelve years of those used the 419 to go to school. In fact I remember the first day of operation of the 419 sometime in 1947. It was quite an event in the village to have a local bus directly to Epsom town. Prior to that it was a long walk up to Epsom Racecourse grandstand to catch a 406.

The first types allocated were the 9T9s and Qs, then a while later 10T10s arrived (still in Green Line livery) and from memory they were in the late 600 and early 700 numbers. Then came the crew RFs, first on Sundays only. It was during the allocation of 10T10s that the service was enhanced to every 20 minutes in the late afternoon, and to help out with this T 448 (a 9T9), overhauled and painted in bus green without white window surrounds, was allocated to LH. This bus is now preserved at Cobham Bus Museum.

I also remember the first day of OMO workings on the 419. It was pouring with rain and the bus, RF 517, had a habit of stalling, which was an extra burden on the driver for this new type service. The 419 was the first route where larger vehicles were tried in OMO. Prior to that only routes with C, CR and GS types were OMO. Coming home in the afternoon the vehicle was RF 700, the very last one made. This vehicle was later experimentally fitted with an electrically driven Setright ticket machine which was mounted on the driver's draught screen. One evening in OMO days we had a GS, covering for an RF failure.

I arrived at Leatherhead bright and early to sign on for duty No. 2 at 5.41am ready for a prompt departure at 5.56, then checked that my money float was adequate; this we had to provide ourselves. Duty 2 had variations for different days of the week, so you had to be awake; today being a Friday you brought back LH 59 from Epsom; Thursdays it was LH 56.

In the canteen the other drivers couldn't understand my enthusiasm to get away, "You don't need twenty minutes to Epsom at this time of day," they said. They were right. By the time I got to Ashtead I was about five minutes up and had to sit there and wait for time. The bus in question was one of the first OMO RFs to be converted, one of the wide cab variety. That early morning cold, and the anticipation, meant a convenience stop was needed behind a suitable woodland site up Wilmerhatch Lane.

Returning on one journey from Brettgrave to Epsom I was aware that someone was over-riding, quite easy to spot really because all of the passengers who boarded at West Park Hospital asked for the same fare, except this one person. My mother was one of the other passengers and she had to see her 'little boy' confront this passenger at the stop before the town centre where his ticket ran out; anyway, I won the day and they paid up.

It was during that first day of being my own boss that another big headache was apparent, i.e. watching the time.

As an aside, the AN I type trained on was AN 24, the same bus that was loaned to the TV series 'On the Buses' and used in the episode where the lead character Stan was being taught on "a new bus" for his garage. He ended up by driving it through an advertising hoarding. A few seconds before this, the LH garage code can plainly be seen on the side of the bus.

WORKING WITH A MATE

The next day, Saturday 16th June 1973 I was to do duty 351 (which also started at 5.41am), a crew job with an old timer as a mate. Charlie had been on the buses for many years and knew all the ropes. Our first job was to extricate our allocated RMC from within the heap; some of the earlier departures hadn't left yet and this made it difficult for us. He said that to get their bus at the front, some of the crews would change the running number plates around in such circumstances, but the Inside Staff get a bit upset, so best not to; not today anyway. After shifting a few we were off towards Kingston. The first half was uneventful; I don't believe I made many mistakes. Les would have been happy with my gear changing, Charlie even remarked that I was a lot smoother and even faster than his regular driver. I felt on top of the World, until returning after our meal break – what did we find?

On arriving back to take our allocated bus, the one in front was still there, well loaded ready for departure but no crew, probably having trouble in travelling there from Leatherhead as passengers on the 71 or 714. Kingston Railway Station bus park is no place you can get a bus to loop round another one; there is only just enough room when everything's right. Charlie was beginning to get a bit upset when I said, "You stand behind and see me back, I will reverse ours back into the entrance of the caravan sales pitch, then we will go out of the entrance, get them all transferred." "What on your third day out? My other mate won't do that, and he's been here for ten years." I don't think I ever lived down that move. We spent the next two weeks as a team and got on really well.

Charlie had two problems. His first caused us a bit of trouble; he couldn't get up in the morning. One morning, whilst waiting for him in the conductors' room, the official shouted, "Rod, your mate's on the phone, he's overslept." He then said, "If you sign for his box, you can run dead to Epsom, and pick him up on the way." There were many buses to Epsom at that time of the morning and he considered that one out wouldn't be missed. Charlie's other "interest" was horse racing, or should I say backing them. At Reigate Station on our way to Redhill he came round and instructed me to wait at Reigate Garage until definitely rung off by him – "don't think I'm busy uptop and go off on your own." As if I would, well not outside Reigate Garage with everyone watching from the main office block. "If anyone comes out of the office and wants to know why you're waiting a long time, tell them I've gone in the garage for something." He was of course across the road in a betting shop. On a return journey he went to pick up his winnings.

Harry Ranger and me with RT 987 at Tadworth station. The photographer asked Harry if he could change the blinds from the 406 to the ones shown, as he didn't have a picture of an RT on that route – Harry said OK but change them back afterwards. *Author's Collection*

HARRY RANGER

The following week Charlie's regular driver returned from holiday and it was then that I was put on the crew rota list and paired with a permanent conductor, namely Harry Ranger. When I was first told of this I felt very apprehensive and a trifle worried; stupid really but that's me; Being a new boy I felt that some of the older blokes could be a bit offish and almost menacing, and thought Harry fitted that. I had often noticed Harry arriving in the car park. He rode one of those old style policeman's bicycles with a "sit up and beg frame" with 28 inch wheels. He had a certain air about him, and like Charlie he had been on the buses for many years. Later he told me he used to drive Green Lines when they were at Leatherhead. Actually my first impressions were so wrong. Harry turned out to be one of the nicest people I have ever met, his first statement being "You'll be all right lad, just do as I tell you, I'll look after you."

The only 'proper' crew route still left at Leatherhead was the 406, but a few other routes were reinforced with trips before or after a 406 run. There was a trip that started at Effingham as a 408 as far as Epsom, and the 462 "rounders" in the evening from Leatherhead roundabout to Fetcham. Harry unlike some of his comrades insisted on having the correct blind displays, including the canopy, for every route.

Right from the start we got on very well, with me being more than content to do just as I was told. From a driver's point of view he was a good mate. His type of ring told you whether we were late or early, and that saved me the job of trying to calculate it from my home made time card in the cab; the conductor had the official one. He never rang you off from upstairs and on RMCs he always rang you off from the only bell, that being situated next to the platform doors close button, this was the message that the conductor would close the doors. If you got a buzzer you knew he/she was somewhere else and the driver must close the doors. If I ever got a buzzer (when with another conductor) I always looked through the bus before doing so, or moving off. When upstairs and near the front, some conductors would stamp on the floor, as a signal to go, but not Harry. Passengers knew and liked him. I was soon dragged into his clan. One day whilst leaving Kingston he rang me off, but I saw this old dear running towards us with a shopping trolley, so I didn't move but looked around to him and pointed. A few stops later there came a sharp knocking on the window behind me. Looking around I saw an apple being passed through the first saloon window, which had been opened to its fullest extent. It was from the lady we had waited for. There were many occasions when we were offered sweets from passengers.

The evening was sunny and the A217 quiet as we stopped at Beechen Lane in Kingswood. He's a long time ringing us off I thought, we're not early. I then noticed him standing alongside the bus miming to me to open my window."I've someone here who wants a word with you," he said with a grin on his face. Harry could have a wicked side at times; what was he up to now? He then produced this rather attractive female. "Claire," I said, "how are you, what are you doing in life?" Claire was someone from my dark past. We were at one time very (in fact extremely) close. Harry said have a chat, "I'll ring us off when it's time." We chatted about nothing in particular, then came the bells and off we set to Redhill.

"That was good of you to let us have a bit of extra time back there," I said, "but what did the passengers think?" "Oh, they were very attentive; I said that you had asked her to marry you, but she hadn't given her answer yet, it was a very crucial moment in your lives, I can't rush them, just another minute." So you see, everyone was happy to sit and watch the outcome. They all agreed that judging by the smiles and waves as you parted that the outcome was a happy one. No wonder passengers were waving bye byes as they passed me. He really excelled with that one, particularly as he knew I was already married with a family.

Some of our old RTs had a good turn of speed. Traffic delays were prevalent on the Kingston Road because of the rebuilding of the railway bridge at Stoneleigh. On one night going toward Kingston we had sat at the lights by the road works for ages. Time was ticking away and we were about five minutes down. We were now in a hurry. At the off the old dear seemed to fly along the dual carriageway, with Harry ringing us through stops where no-one was waiting. The speedo read 53 at one time. "Grand piece of driving," Harry said later, "obviously left over from your motor cycling days."

This rushing around to get back on time nearly came unstuck one day in the rain. Coming up through Ewell village to the lights where the route went right, and with me going a touch too fast, the RT had other ideas and tried to go straight on; it took all my strength to get it round. At the Tadworth turn I examined the front tyres. They were impersonating 'slicks' usually found on racing cars!

The other piece of rushing around and coming unstuck occurred on a Saturday. The week before we had been severely 'slaughtered' in that on leaving Kingston the passenger loadings were heavy, and the delay this caused was compounded by traffic hold ups. It didn't help that we had left late because of our problems in travelling there from Leatherhead on the 714. In consequence we arrived at Redhill about ten minutes down.

So the next week on the journey half an hour later, we managed to get out of Kingston sharp, and went like a bat out of hell. Success at Epsom, two minutes up, but there was still a long way to go. Harry rang us off straight away. The Epsom–Redhill section was very unpredictable; on a quiet day you could make up a good eight minutes, on a bad day the reverse, and on a Saturday the single carriageway A217 could get very busy. It was a hot day and the RT was not one of the best and took a bit of pushing to get it along. After Epsom town there is a long hill leading up to the Downs and the old girl was struggling in 2nd on the last bit.

It was as we pulled up at the Grandstand stop that I first realised something was wrong, when the radiator cap started to dance about. It was a quick shut of the cab window before the cap lifted a bit and steam billowed out. I switched off and jumped out and, before Harry could stop me, I had undone the cap fully with a rag I kept in the cab. He came up behind and whispered "Silly boy, you should have kept going – it would have died down on its own; anyway not much has come out, we'll fill it at Redhill."

I wasn't too sure about this advice, partly because Harry had never owned a car and also if it blew up it would have been me for the high jump. Water in the radiator was the driver's responsibility. Experience later showed he was right. I should have remembered his first introduction days earlier, "Just do as I tell you, I'll look after you."

Luck was with us. No traffic, no passengers and the level crossing at Reigate was open for a change. At Reigate Station we were four minutes early and duly met by an inspector hiding behind the stop enquiring of me as to why we were such. I leant through the window and told him of our journey and of last week. His answer was, "You can't win them all you know" and waived us off.

That boil up got my mind working. I remembered reading in one of the traffic circulars a section on watering points and on finding it, discovered I was right, there was one half way up Ashley Road, next to a shed behind the memorial in the cemetery. The next Sunday when it was quiet, I stopped and checked. Sure enough there was a tap and an old watering can with 'LT' on it. Apparently the real purpose of the tap was for people to water the plants on graves.

THE MORNING RUSH

In the morning rush there were four departures from Tadworth to Kingston between 7.48 and 8.12. Passenger loadings and road traffic were very heavy all along the route, causing some bunching and in consequence a lot of 'leap-frogging' of the buses occurred. This was standard practice with a lot of the crews who generally helped each other out.

Harry had two reservations concerning the matter though. Firstly, if we spotted anyone deliberately hanging back behind not doing their share then we must let them catch up. There was one crew who were well known for this; it was a driver and his girlfriend clippie. And as the story goes, one morning this hanging about was noticed by the driver of the bus in front, who himself hung about a bit until they closed up, with the result that at the roundabout at Tolworth he went round it twice and then came out behind the offender, who hadn't guessed what was happening until it was too late.

Harry's second concern was that it was important that we all go up the final straight to Kingston station in the correct order, especially those going into the station stand; otherwise you couldn't get out in the right order.

One of the five, LH 2 on duty 309, didn't go into the station bus stand, but dumped passengers outside and then proceeded to Norbiton London Transport Garage where it was later joined by another, LH 7 on duty 302, and where both 'slept' until 14.40 for LH 2 and at 13.10 for LH 7. After parking the bus at Norbiton you walked back to Kingston where either you had a meal break or continued your duty on another bus.

One of the next terminating buses went back to Leatherhead on a dead run. It was whilst driving on this run that I was bombarded with a series of bells. Looking around I saw an irate passenger waving his hands at Harry. This passenger had quietly jumped on while we were at some traffic lights and then panicked when we deviated from the 406 route at Ditton Road to the 65 for the short cut back to Leatherhead. At the time Harry was busy sitting at the front of the bus engrossed in his Waybill. "Read the blinds dear passenger, it may say 406 but the via points say Private and the ultimate is blank."

Harry and I had a mutual dislike, and that was the parking of cars in designated bus bays. One site where we managed to get our own back was Tadworth Station which was very convenient for short time shoppers, who on returning found their exit blocked by a big bus. Their question put to Harry of "how long before you go?" was usually answered by, "In about ten minutes and the driver is around the corner and won't be back until then."

1st June 1975 saw RF 655 standing in for an SM on an LH Sunday allocation on route 406. Photographed outside Reigate garage it looks as if it is being replenished with water, as the radiator cap is off. *Roy Hobbs collection*

The Sunday allocation on the 406 was three single deck OPO vehicles. LH provided two SM vehicles, and RG one MB type. MBS 91 is on the stand at Kingston. *Ian Pringle*

LIFE CONTINUES

For about ten minutes we had been sitting in our dimly lit bus at Tadworth turn after completing what nowadays is considered a dangerous move, i.e., crossing two electrified railway lines by way of the old porter's walkboards. Tadworth railway station had a gents toilet, but it was on the other side platform, and crossing the track that way was quicker than walking across the bridge and down the slope. "Time to hit the road" came my instruction from Harry. "Yes Sir," I obeyed. Up in the cab, pull the starter and 'thud', try again, saloon lights dim but no go. Turning all the lights off and trying a minute later produced the same effect. "Will take them about an hour to wake up and get out here this time of night," states Harry. I had this idea – we still have air up, why not bump start – should work. "But we're facing up the hill" said Harry. "Never mind that, this is a quiet road. To be safe, you go back a bit and keep a lookout. I will lean out of the cab and watch for your signal." I selected reverse, held the operating pedal down, released the handbrake and off we went backwards. A little speed was all that was wanted to lock up the flywheel, on lifting the pedal it started and we were back in business again. "In all my years I've never seen that done before," he said. "You can only do it if you've got air up," I said, sounding like an expert. Some time back I had wondered if it was possible to do that, and had proved it was with an empty RF one afternoon on the downhill section of Beaconsfield Road in Langley Vale when on the 419.

In fact we did that very same thing the next week at the Redhill Station turn, but this time in an RMC and we were going forward. That time I should have guessed something was amiss, as when we took over the bus in Kingston the engine had been left running.

Many occasions when paired with Harry I had been diverted to one-man duties, and gratefully accepted this because of the enhanced pay. Harry did not like this much; in our short partnership we had become a good team and it now meant he was working with all sorts.

Before we finally parted, I was invited to meet his wife Enid, who was equally as pleasant. At the door I was greeted by this beautifully dressed female of about twenty. "Who was that?" I asked Harry when she was out of earshot. "My daughter," he replied. "I didn't know you had a daughter, let alone one who could fill a dress that well," I said. "I know I didn't tell you" came his reply. "Actually there are two more as well" – "Three like that?" "Yep, and they're all a good bunch," said Enid as she entered the room.

Harry was also a keen gardener and owned five allotments and often would bring bags of his vegetable produce for his colleagues. There were times when the conductors' room looked more like a market stall.

There is one type of driving you weren't taught and that was night driving. This was a bit of an oversight as many of the roads have very poor lighting and RT and original RF lights are none too clever. Where are the lights?, I thought jumping up into the RT cab in the dark and then quickly being given the off. Apart from a cursory glance during type training I hadn't much bothered with them, as up till then all my driving had been on 'earlies'. The small torch in my bag proved invaluable. In fact one evening another tool also came in handy, namely a small adjustable spanner. Now one asks, why carry these? It goes back to auntie's boyfriend who said he always took a torch, a small screwdriver to tighten up the interior mirrors on OMO buses plus a small adjustable spanner to hold the back nut. And for jammed ticket machines you will need tweezers. On picking up an RT at Kingston I was aware of the excessive smell of diesel and she was a bit 'chuffy'. At Tadworth turn, a quick look under the bonnet revealed a loose injector pipe. The adjustable spanner my wife had bought me came into use here. She assured me it was a multi-purpose one – it fitted both imperial and metric nuts and as usual she was right.

The overheating of RTs up to Epsom Downs was quite common. "It is your driving technique," argued a big headed new driver in the canteen during one of his "I've done everything better than you" sessions. "It has never happened to me" he boasted. Somehow it became known that he was to take over the worst culprit for steaming, and whilst in Kingston, without him knowing, the radiator was duly treated to a few cupfulls of washing up liquid. According to his conductor on the day when the top blew off at the Grandstand, the front of the bus could not be seen for rusty coloured foam. This incident served two purposes: firstly it reduced his head size a fraction and secondly the fitters asked what had been done to it, as the overheat problem appeared cured.

For a very short while MBS 4, one of the original prototypes, was allocated to LH. It is seen here at Epsom station on a 481 swinger. *Ian Pringle*

For a driver, going over Epsom Downs had another problem. The road between Tattenham Corner and the Grandstand was very exposed to the elements, particularly when going in the direction of Epsom, and if the wind was up it took a fair bit of opposite lock to hold the bus straight. When you got to the Grandstand though, this magnificent building acted as a grand windbreak and all the side wind was suddenly blocked, meaning that the opposite lock wasn't required anymore. If you didn't take it off quickly the bus had a tendency to go into the Grandstand, about a foot from the road.

A SCRAPE, BUT JUST ONCE
The turn in West Croydon bus station could be a bit tight at times because there was only just enough room to do the required complete 'U' turn, and if another bus was parked near the stand it meant a little reverse shunt to get round, which wasn't too bad as the visibility was quite good. The bus station by Kingston Station though was another kettle of fish and was not one of my favourites. To get the maximum number of buses in, the marked lanes had been brought quite close to the railings by the inspector's hut, meaning that a lot of lock was required to get out and, because the next lane was very close, extreme care was needed especially with SMs and MBs. The original design of the stand went back many years when buses were a lot shorter and narrower, with STs, STLs and Ts being the regular users. Now we had SMSs on the 85 next to the rail fence, with the 406 sandwiched between SMs on the 418 and DMSs on the 213, both of which had the habit of often pulling right up tight and crooked. To our left the driver of the SM on the 418 had done just that, to give himself plenty of room on his nearside so he didn't clout the 85 with his rear overhang when he wound on the lock. He was so close, passengers were cleaning the sides of both buses as they squeezed through to our bus. Between us and the DMS on the 213 was a narrow area for the 213 queue. This was an excellent idea I'm sure waiting passengers really appreciated, as when you started your bus and revved it up to get up air you plastered them all with mucky diesel fumes. Also if you needed water for the radiator, it meant forcing a gap in the queue to get to the standpipe, which was situated on the outer wall. And on the return, there was a chance of slopping water over them from the can.

Recognising me as a newish driver with probably little experience of this type of situation and seeing me squeeze into the cab, the inspector came out of his hut to assist me. Pointing to the left or right to guide me through the gap I was watching his directions carefully when a heavy banging on the cab rear window stopped me in my tracks. Looking round I saw this female passenger pointing and shouting to the right side of our bus. On leaning from the door I could see we were making a nice graze along our bus with the DMS mirror. "Don't worry," said the inspector, "it's only a scratch, forget it." It may only be a scratch to him I thought, but to me, it's my pride. From that I learnt, never trust somebody who is guiding you, always check as well.

I wasn't the only one who was having a scrape. My close buddy from training days, Little Dave as Harry named him for obvious reasons, came into the limelight again. I believe Dave was the one who refused to work with one of the older clippies, as he said she tried to abuse him one night in his cab while on the Tadworth stand (lucky Dave). His next claim to fame was not particularly pleasant for him. During type training we were continuously made aware of the long overhang on SM vehicles. It seems that Dave forgot this, and whilst coming into a tight bus bay, in his effort to get the bus close to the curb, the front overhang caught the bus shelter and changed its location slightly. His excuse was that he didn't do much OMO work and had become unfamiliar with the SM, and it was accepted.

The fact that I did more OMO work also meant that I had the other headache of balancing the waybill at the end of the shift and dealing with obstinate ticket machines, which I was convinced had a mind of their own – they always chose to jam at the most inconvenient moment; they just weren't capable of doing it at a quiet time. My worst was on a busy evening return in the semi dark, and ended with me sitting with the torch in my mouth and the tweezers pulling out the fold behind the guillotine of an Almex II, eagerly watched by the first few on the steps. It was either do that or get out the emergency pack of individual tickets, which was more hassle than fixing the machine.

When using the emergency ticket pack, a separate waybill had to be filled out for them as well as the normal one. If the machine persisted in jamming you could, if passing the garage, ask for a replacement, which again required a second waybill. In any case I always reported any jamming; sometimes it was caused by just a build up of dust behind the guillotine. I seem to remember that one could claim extra time for filling in second waybills.

Right Gibson Waybill, showing that it referred to two issues of that same machine (usually to the same conductor two days running). As can be seen, the readings for each denomination were required, and this necessitated some mental arithmetic when 'cashing up' at the end of duty. Hence the allowance of ten minutes to do so.

CASH TOTAL SHEET
LONDON COUNTRY BUS SERVICES LTD.
GIBSON TICKET MACHINES

MACHINE No.	DUTY NUMBER	
	1st Day	2nd Day
_u_	W	2

GARAGE **REIGATE** T/C .... 22 / .... 1st DAY DATE
23 / .... 2nd DAY DATE

REGISTER READINGS			Quantity sold	Value	Quantity sold	1st DAY		2nd DAY	
CLOSE of 2nd Day	CLOSE of 1st Day	START of 1st Day	1st Day	P	2nd Day	£	p	£	p
1 7 5	1 2 7	0 4 2	85	15	48	12	75	7	20
2 1	0 7 0	0 4 4	26	2	51		52	1	02
7 6 3	7 5 8	7 3 0	28	3	05		84		15
1 4 7	0 4 8	0 2 5	23	4	99		92	3	96
1 1 1	0 5 0	0 0 0	50	5	61	2	50	3	05
1 2 2	1 0 9	0 6 8	41	6	13	2	46		78
2 7 3	2 3 2	1 7 2	60	7	41	4	20	2	87
4 3 6	4 0 4	3 8 4	2 0	8	32	1	60	2	56
4 0 0	3 7 1	3 4 6	25	9	29	2	25	2	61
1 0 0	0 5 7	9 9 6	61	10	43	6	10	4	30
4 4 5	4 4 4	4 3 8	06	1	01	0	6	0	1
5 4 7	5 4 0	5 3 0	1 0	1½	07	1	5		10½
3 1 3	2 7 9	2 4 7	32	2½	34		80		85
6 2 5	5 9 6	5 8 1	1 5	7½	29	1	12½	2	17½
				TOTAL		36	27	31	64
				Parcel Labels					

Emergency tickets (Brought forward)

Compiled by	GRAND TOTAL		

OFFICIAL'S USE 26.	OFFICIAL'S USE		TOTAL REGISTER READINGS	Record-ed by (Initials)	FARE REGISTER READINGS and PARCEL LABELS checked by
		CLOSE of 1st day			
		CLOSE of 2nd day			

Day	Conductor's name (block letters)	Driver's name (block letters)	Number
1st			

UP A GRADE

The usual direct promotion open to a crew bus driver was to an OMO driver, and although there had been many occasions when instead of working with Harry I had been seconded to OMO driving for a day, the pay increase was only paid for that time. When that happened Harry's driver would have been a non OMO driver possibly on overtime. If you were classified as an OMO driver, you received that enhanced rate all the time, even if you did crew driving.

The usual gang of newish drivers were drinking tea one day discussing the one promotion displayed on 'the board' all saying that Roy (who was not with us then) would get it as he had the seniority and therefore automatically got preference over anyone else. I was half watching the television at this point and missed this bit of the conversation so I was ignorant of the rules. On the way out I asked the office for the correct form and duly filled it in applying for the post. To everyone's amazement I was given the promotion, Roy later said he didn't want OMO work and therefore didn't apply. The others, all with more seniority than me, didn't bother to apply as they assumed Roy would go for it; still there were no hard feelings.

Harry was not over happy, as we had become a good team and it meant he had to start training a new mate and there were some candidates that he had great reservations about! But as it turned out Little Dave asked for the position as he really didn't like OMO work. Harry was quite happy as on occasions they had worked together before.

This meant that I was transferred back to the OMO instructions rota (which I liked) and did hardly any more crew work, which I found a bit of a bore anyway. I found OMO work more interesting because of the direct contact with the passengers, something I quite enjoyed. However, because my

Facing page This OMO duty schedule sheet shows how duty No. 2 changed with different days of the week. This if my memory is correct is because the 419 ran a different service on Thursday to take account of the visiting arrangements at the nearby mental hospitals. Also quite evident is how varied each day could be with different routes and different vehicle types being the norm. The * against a duty time told you that after then was either a meal break or the start of the spread-over break. Although a "spread" made it a long day, you also got paid for about three hours forty minutes when actually you weren't at work. The letter code underneath the duty number referred to the pay rate for that particular duty. The lowest rate (A) was for RF, then came SM (B), and the highest (C) was for ANs. A mixed duty was paid at the higher or highest rate.

These sheets only gave the times that an individual did for that duty and the relevant running numbers. When on the bus of that running number, another card gave what that bus was supposed to do. Using that information along with a timetable you had to work out the actual times of the bus at the various timed points along the route. You had to be careful not to over-run your bit, or else you could end up doing part of someone else's duty.

Duties started fifteen minutes before taking over or travelling on the first bus. During this time you checked the issue of your machine etc. Crew bus conductors were only given ten minutes. Likewise at the end of duty these were the times given to complete the waybill, 'cash up', and hand it all to the depot office.

Duty	Start	Route	Run No	Time	Place	Time	Place	Finish
1	05.41	470	LH 12	05.56	LH	09.13	LL *	
C		408	11	09.59	LN	13.23	LI	13.48
2	05.41	419	LH 55	05.56	LH	10.16	EM	
A	MTWF	EMPTY	59	10.22	ET	10.38	LH *	
	MTWF	EMPTY	59	11.22	LH	11.37	ET	
	Th	EMPTY	56	10.22	ET	10.38	LH *	
	Th	EMPTY	56	11.22	LH	11.37	ET	
		468	61	11.41	ET	13.09	ET	
		EMPTY	62	13.17	ET	13.33	LH	13.48
3	05.51	408	LH 18	06.06	LH	09.23	LI *	
C			19	10.23	LI	13.39	LN	13.54
4	05.52	418	LH 31	06.07	LH	08.36	LL *	
b			32	09.44	LN	13.14	LN	13.29
5	05.53	468	LH 62	06.08	LH	09.52	LH *	
B		462	57	10.41	LN	11.02	LL	
		418	35	11.14	LN	13.56	LL	14.11
6	05.54	468	LH 14	06.09	LH	06.38	LN	
C		470	20	06.51	LH	10.09	LH *	
		408	12	10.59	LN	13.34	LD	13.59
7	06.06	416	LH 51	06.21	LH	09.42	LH *	
C		470	GF 1	10.34	LD	13.58	LL	14.13
8	06.15	418	LH 32	06.30	LH	09.44	LN *	
B			34	10.44	LN	14.14	LN	14.29
9	06.20	408	LH 13	06.35	LH	10.23	LL *	
C		470	GF 2	11.34	LD	14.58	LL	15.13
10	06.20	408	LH 19	06.35	LH	10.23	LI*	
C		470	12	13.34	LD	17.04	LD	17.29
11	06.24	481	LH 27	06.39	LH	09.29	LH*	
C		408	13	10.23	LL	14.34	LD	14.59
12	06.27	418	LH 35	06.42	LH	11.14	LN *	
C		408	22	13.54	LH	16.34	LD	16.59
13	06.34	418	LH 33	06.49	LH	10.14	LN *	
B			40	14.51	LH	18.42	LN	18.57
14	06.40	408	LH 24	06.55	LH	11.04	LH *	
C			18	12.39	LN	15.18	LL	15.33
15	06.41	416	LH 52	06.56	LH	09.50	LH *	
C		408	15	14.09	LN	18.27	LH	18.42
16	06.53	416	LH 53	07.08	LH	08.58	LH	
C		408	GF 2	09.04	LN	11.34	LD *	
		416	LH 51	13.32	LH	15.34	LH	15.49
17	06.53	416	LH 63	07.08	LH	08.59	ET	
C		EMPTY	21	09.03	ET	09.19	LH *	
		470	13	14.34	LD	19.02	LH	19.17
18	06.54	470	LH 15	07.09	LH	09.39	LN *	
C		418	34	14.14	LN	18.58	LH	19.13

The place codes are as follows: LH = Leatherhead Garage, LN = Leatherhead Garage (north), LL = Leatherhead Garage (south), LD = Leatherhead Crescent, LI = Leatherhead Institute, ET = Epsom Station.

job mainly entailed driving buses that were generally filling in for gaps or late running, I often became the brunt of their moans. These generally I could quite understand, except when they became rude and personal. On these occasions there was a great temptation to reply in a similar vein. But somehow I always managed to hold my cool and explain the situation how it was (traffic delays always went down well) and that I was a relief driver brought in to try to sort out the service. This approach usually worked, but not always, and if they persisted with the discussion, I usually asked what did they want me to do, continue arguing with them and cause further delays, or get on and drive the bus? I sometimes added that I was being paid overtime at that moment so I didn't mind either.

SOME MIXED EVENTS

Race days at Epsom were a big strain on the system, both with vehicles and staff. I was due at the garage around 11.00, supposedly to do a middle shift on the 408, but on arrival was asked if I minded changing as my services were more needed for the races. They could get my job covered in bits by three others. Sounds interesting, I thought, and it will give me a chance to see if there are any unusual vehicles up there. "Go to Epsom, report to the controller by the station and tell him I sent you," were my instructions.

At Epsom it looked total chaos with buses in long queues, passengers fighting to get on them and only a few crews to be seen. First question from this rather harassed looking gent was, "Do I know the way to the Downs, the turning point and way back?". That may seem a bit silly, but on race days a system was in operation that made Ashley Road one way to the races in the morning and the opposite way later for returning traffic. The return in the morning was via the very narrow Chalk Lane, barely wide enough for a bus in the lower section. It also had the added problem that one of the race stables was situated halfway down it, so when careering back in the morning with an empty bus one had to be careful not to collide with a potential Derby winner being led up to the races. This lane I knew well, it was my cycle route to Epsom. On a normal day it would be quiet, it being restricted to 'access only' vehicles. In fact being born and brought up only half a mile from the Derby start, I knew nearly every nook and cranny on the Downs and having travelled home from school that way on race days was quite familiar with the turning arrangements. In those days the normal bus on the 406 was an RT, but race days we would wait for an interesting bus drafted in from another shed to come round for the trip, something like a front entrance STL, but that was in about 1951. On race days, the 419 that usually took me home was suspended, and so was the normal 406. The only way for me to get home was to go to 'The Downs' by the 'specials', and then walk to Langley Vale. The half fare on the specials was 3d whereas on the normal route it was 2d. However if I complained to the conductor I usually got away with the normal fare.

RT 2157, later to become the seat store behind LH garage, is seen here making the tight turn into Tattenham Corner in July 1976. This tight curve combined with a slope took some heaving to pull a loaded RT around. I usually slowed right down and engaged 2nd gear just before the turn. If you took it too fast, because of the angle of the loaded bus, there was a possibility of scraping the end of the exhaust on the road. Note the use of 'side blinds' in the front 'via' position; this was becoming a common practice. The bus shelter to the right behind the bus was for the other direction, and not in a very safe location. To turn right and join the main road was not always easy and then you may have to immediately stop.
Colin Fradd

The first bus in the line was already full and ready for the off with the conductor already busy collecting fares. "Take that for a few rounders," he said, "Can't" said I, "not been type trained on RCLs." (It may sound silly, but RMC type training didn't cover RCLs). "Look you're a clever chap, I'm sure you can manage that extra few inches, do me a favour and go."

So I type trained myself on RCLs and I suppose RMLs. The RCL was a beautiful bus, so comfortable and with a bit more power than the RMC. After that day I never drove one again. Reigate had an allocation of both RCLs and RMLs, but because of the tight clearance under Stoneleigh railway bridge they were both restricted past Ewell to Kingston.

It was thought that because the road dipped under the bridge, the extra length could cause the bus to catch the bridge on entry or exit. A section in a traffic circular stated that RMC vehicles were limited to 20mph under that bridge, the reason being that the air suspension might allow the vehicle to bounce. There were however stories of RTs with new springs apparently touching the bridge. The only allocation of RCL/RML on the 406 was a morning school days only journey from Tattenham Corner to Redhill and that was a Reigate duty.

Serviceable vehicles were getting quite a problem, with often an afternoon AN allocation on the Chessington Zoo to Epsom 'shorts' on the 468 being

This is a very unusual substitute for an AN, particularly as the 470 was run by LH, who did not have an allocation of RCLs. According to the garage code, RCL 2246 was allocated to Chelsham (CM), hence the very makeshift blinds. The location is Dorking bus garage forecourt. *Ian Pringle*

covered by an RT. This duty I did many times as 'Odd Job', and was often paired with the same clippie for the occasion. Vera, who was married to another driver, had spent many years on the buses and was a lovely person. A crew bus running to an OMO timetable had plenty of time for the run. Vera managed to pad it out by giving extra help to the mothers with push chairs and the loads of young kids returning from a Zoo visit.

Another piece of customer service was the special stop made when traversing Epsom Downs in the late evening and was for those returning from the pubs in Epsom. After leaving The Grandstand stop, if you got five bells it was the signal to stop at the toilet mid-way between stops on the Downs.

During training you were told to always check the nearside mirror when pulling away from a stop and eventually it became an automatic action. In doing this late one night in an RT, I spied someone running at great knots to catch us; poor devil I thought as I applied the brakes, we'll wait. The next thing was four rings on the bell, an emergency stop message. Leaving the cab and going round to see the trouble I was met by a blood-stained man. Running at a good speed he had made a giant leap for the bus, but not reckoned on it slowing down and in consequence had hit his face on the centre pole. His nose was bleeding profusely but he refused medical attention. The stopping of a bus after leaving a stop is against the regulations, so in slowing down for him I was committing an offence.

Luggage was allowed but the rules concerning the size of it were a bit vague. Stopping to pick up outside Leatherhead Post Office on an early evening 416 journey to Boxhill, I was confronted by two gents in their mid-twenties with the request could they bring their luggage aboard? "What was it?" I asked. The two bits of wood about eight feet long and a sink bowl weren't going to fit via the normal entrance, so it was open up the rear emergency door of the RF and slide the goods in from there. The wood slid along the floor and one of the gents held the sink unit from his rear seat. At Boxhill the process was reversed; quite easy really.

"WHAT DO *YOU* KNOW ABOUT BUSES?"
Unlike many people, I had a good two-way relationship with the office; we did each other favours. Several times when I was off, the phone would ring with a request from the office – could I go in and do half a duty. In return they would change my rest day if the need arose.

It was about this time that I was caught by the chief with a fitter playing with an SM which apparently had an intermittent "no gears" problem, but you could get gears with the circuit breaker turned off, so the main select and electro-pneumatic system was OK. With the circuit breaker off it allowed you to drive the bus with the doors open, but you lost control of the doors on the door buttons, so you had to control them via the taps. The chief asked the fitter what was I doing in the shed, apparently out of bounds to drivers, and then turned and asked me, "What do you know about f***ing buses?"

Vehicle availability became so poor in 1974 and 1975 that several were hired in from other operators. London Transport provided many MBSs, which unlike their LCBS counterparts were fitted with fully automatic transmission. MBS 124 represents one of them. *Ian Pringle*

Advert bus RMC 1490 at the Redhill terminus of the 406. *Ian Pringle*

After studying the system diagram I suggested that he look at the door inter-lock switches – it turned out to be a good guess.

It then became apparent to the Chief that I knew more about the subject than the two of them, but this only was because the company had not given them adequate training. In comparison, I had studied electronics to degree standard, and prior to my turning to electronics had spent three years as a toolmaker so therefore had a good mechanical background also. When quiet, I often used to wander around to see what was happening.

We had this single door AN which everyone complained about being slow. I understood that the injectors and the fuel pump had been changed and that the heads were next on the list. An afternoon journey to Dorking and back meant that I was given this machine. It was strange. There was no power and at the same time there was no black smoke, the revs seemed to limit very low down. Sitting at Dorking with my foot on the accelerator, I had a feeling that the pedal movement was limited, and going to another bus on the stand my diagnosis was confirmed. On return to Leatherhead not wishing to look like a know-all or be ridiculed if wrong (like "mind your own business, just drive the bus"), I spoke again in secret to my friendly fitter. Later he admit-ted I was right; all that was wrong with the bus was that the throttle stop under the pedal had been set too high, which stopped the pedal from going right down and therefore stopped the fuel pump from fully opening. To cure the fault all he did was to adjust the bolt to shorten it!

A BRUSH WITH OFFICIALDOM
Inspectors themselves could have funny turns, and at times they couldn't see when you were trying your best.

I was working a rest day, and in setting up the blinds in Kingston for the 418A journey to Leatherhead in an SM it became apparent that although the front blind had the correct number and ultimate destination, the rear blind only had 418. There was only one 'A' variety return journey and it went via the main road between Ashtead and Leatherhead and not via the Lower Road. This could be confusing I decided. If anyone boards from behind they will think I'm a normal 418, so what else have we? The decision to show 408 which went the same way as a 418A after Epsom was my choice, but not that of the inspector watching my departure from Kingston. He rushed up to the door and banged furiously on it until I stopped. He then threatened to report me for sloppy blinds. Not taking this very kindly I decided to beat him to it, and on my return to Leatherhead asked for an audience with the Garage Traffic Superintendent. I agreed that between Kingston and Epsom the blind showed a route not running over that section, but that was better than having people on the wrong bus after Epsom. This he accepted as the best move and said he would "have a talk with the inspector about his attitude". On another occasion, about mid-afternoon, I was 'jumped' near West Ewell – nothing unusual except that when I was asked to sign his sheet, the time stated was some hours off the real time. When I queried this I was told "Just shut up and sign it, I need some time to do some shopping, OK".

To increase revenue, London Country introduced a strange policy for children's fares. Instead of half, children were to be charged approximately two thirds of the adult fare. This was not popular with staff as the complicated arrangement required major mathematics or consultation of the fare chart for the correct fare on most occasions, and was usually followed by abuse from passengers about the increase. On one such occasion a woman with five children of fare-paying age boarded my bus. On hearing the new amount, she almost burst into tears saying she didn't have enough money and how could she get home with all her shopping and her "brood". I could have asked her to fill in an unpaid fares form, but my reaction was like many of my colleagues; "what a rather silly system". Instead, I said, "Just pay for two and go and sit down". That cheered her up a bit, a bus driver with a bit of heart. It cheered me up a bit also, but not for long.

A few stops on, and what have we got here? The jumper who made me sign his forged time sheet a few days earlier. When I informed him that I knew there was a passenger on my bus having not paid the fare (in fact there were three) his face lit up for the kill. "This will look good on your record lad," he hissed as he started to fill in the relevant details. "I wonder," I said, "if it's as bad as fiddling time sheets? You do of course still remember the other afternoon?" Uttering abuse he hurriedly got off at the next stop.

One Sunday morning after leaving Redhill bound for Kingston with my delightful SM, at the first stop in the one-way system was a Reigate inspector; strange I thought, they're up early for a Sunday. Anyway he quizzed me as to whether I had seen any passengers who looked as if they were bound for a day out to the coast, as the coach was waiting and already late. At the next stop, low and behold were quite a few passengers, a lot more than usual for a Sunday, the first of whom mounted my bus and asked if I had seen a tour coach, which should have been there ten minutes ago. Now I can be quite bright at times and connected the two incidents. "Your coach is waiting for you round the other end of the one-way system," I informed them. "How far's that?" came the question. These folk were of the type one would expect on a day trip to the coast, pensioners and their sisters and not the type who could do a quick dash around Redhill.

"I tell you what, get on and I'll take you round." So on they got and off we went round the one-way system to where the coach was waiting. On seeing me again, the by-that-time not very happy inspector jumped on and said, "What are you doing back here?" "Your passengers were round at the next stop so I decided to bring them for you," I said. He soon realised I had helped him, and then thanked me. Making up five minutes on a Sunday morning on a ninety-minute trip was no hard chore.

The second 406 duty on a Sunday meant that after your meal break in Kingston you took over RG 32 to which an MB was allocated. If Reigate were short they would sub it with an RF. Not this day though. The sub was a National. What a delightful change this will make I decided as I boarded my steed for the next three and a half hours. The preceding driver had left the blinds correctly set for my return so all that was left was to set up the machine, fill in the waybill, load up the two passengers and go. "Not so fast sonny" came the voice of the same dear inspector who some weeks earlier had objected to my choice of blind display.

"You can't drive this, you're not type trained. I will drive it, you can take the fares." "How do you know I am not type trained?" "Because no Leatherhead drivers are." "So are you type trained, you're a Leatherhead Inspector?" He didn't like that bit. Quickly I said I had been type trained during initial training and if he didn't believe me, he should consult the training record at Reigate. The trip to Redhill and back passed without incident, but I wasn't over-sure about the new buses with their thin rexine seats.

As the last passenger got off my SM on a 418 in Clarence Street, Kingston she mentioned that a package had been left on the rear seat. We were at that time deeply into the suspect package era. Anyway, as I was empty I decided to continue to the next stop which was the terminus, where there should be an inspector. Against procedures the brave inspector decided to investigate the package, whereupon he announced that all was clear as it contained several peaches which he proceeded to eat as they were perishables and any such found on a vehicle should be destroyed. On the return journey a young lady boarded at West Ewell and said she had left a package on my bus and had I found it. My approximately truthful reply of it being destroyed didn't please her, but she changed her tune when I reminded her of the chaos it could have created if we had followed procedures and probably evacuated all of Kingston.

On some nights an unofficial procedure was used which did contain a lot of sense. Kingston around five o'clock was a mad house and the traffic was such that in the slow moving traffic approaching C & A corner, if you looked in your mirror you could often see the next one, supposedly 10 minutes behind you. If in Kingston bus station you were ready and full with a standing load, you would frequently get the off from the inspector even if it wasn't time yet. These few minutes were very useful in that traffic.

We seemed to be having more of our share of rain that week and I was doing a few more late turns. On the way into Leatherhead with my empty SM on the 418 I just fancied a nice bag of hot chips thinking they would go well with my flask of tea when I got to Bookham Station, so it was a quick nip out at the fish shop in Kingston Road, which even with a bit of preferential treatment still took a few minutes. Then it was full pelt towards the garage just in case Mr Jumper was still awake. Because of "no right turn" at the traffic lights, the route to the garage meant you had to go all round the one way system – left at the lights just past the post office, up the High

Street, sharp right into The Crescent, then right at the end and then left at the lights you had passed some minutes earlier into Bridge Street. There were stories of some drivers cheating late at night and doing an unlawful right turn directly into Bridge Street. Anyway almost skidding to a halt as the lights changed at that junction, I was aware of a figure who came out of a shop doorway. It was Mr Plod, who banged on the door beckoning me to open it. "In a rush tonight are we Sir?" "Yes Officer we're a bit late." "Oh well never mind, give me a lift to Bookham Church!"

Conductors could be very good at sorting out disruptions to the service, all on their own without the intervention of an Inspector. One Saturday afternoon our first trip was to take over a 406 in Epsom, and we travelled there on a normal service 408 from Leatherhead. Actually the official changeover place for buses in the Kingston direction was in the High Street outside 'The Charter Inn' and coded 'EI', but it was always done in Ashley Road, one stop back, outside the register office where the traffic was lighter.

On changeovers, it was a requirement that you stayed with the bus until the taking-over crew arrived. Ten minutes after the booked time an RT appeared, but not ours. Charlie "the racing fanatic", enquired of the conductor "Problems today Mate?" "Yep, traffic in Kingston is worse than ever today because of Summer Sales" he said, as two more pulled up behind, the second of the next pair being ours. Soon there were five 406s there blocking Ashley Road. There followed a short discussion between the five conductors, with the result that I was told we were going 'dead' via the quicker 418 route to Ruxley Lane, and then on to Tolworth where we went back in service. One of the others went 'dead' all the way to Kingston. At Kingston the Inspector was quite happy that his service had been recovered, a bit anyway.

RF 79 seen here leaving Epsom in September 1977 is acting as a 'sub' for an SM. This vehicle was later converted and became the engineer's bus. *Colin Fradd*

THE WRONG ROAD

Because of the nature of what I did, i.e. working under instructions, there were many occasions when I didn't take the normal route, but there were other times when I should have done – I wasn't alone in that.

My first morning on conductor training was on a 406 from Leatherhead garage to Tadworth, which in Epsom – because of a no right turn at the main traffic lights into Ashley Road – was supposed to go round the back of the station. Our driver though went down past the clock tower and made this unauthorised turn; he apparently always did it. At 6.30 in the morning who's there to see him.

And there were others. One of the morning journeys on the 462 from Leatherhead to Chertsey, Barker Road, was fraught with delays. School kids through Fetcham, traffic through Cobham, heavy loadings to the old BAC works, and worse more traffic past the Ship Pub in Weybridge. No-one it seemed could keep the bus on time, except 'Little Dave'. On returning to the Leatherhead canteen after one such 462 journey, I slumped down in the chair and Dave asked how did I manage to get so late; he had had no trouble? There followed a discussion on what happened where, and how late each bit made you. It then transpired how he managed to run more to time. At Weybridge Station he went straight on, instead of going right. This shortcut missed the Ship pub stop and all of Weybridge High Street; how he didn't get complaints I don't know.

It was while on a late evening 408 that I really did get lost. This particular duty had a long layover in Commercial Road, Guildford, and the Company in their wisdom thought it too long to stay on the stand, so they decided the bus and driver should go to Guildford garage – the one in that narrow road which you notice just as you drive past it, just as I did – very vague that bit. Somehow in the panic that followed, suddenly I was on the A3 going towards Portsmouth. Anyway up the hill just by the Hogs Back turning I did a U turn and traced my steps back again.

Then I did a classic one on a Sunday 406 coming out of Kingston. Leatherhead's Sunday allocation on the 406 were two SMs, the same type as the weekday allocation on the 418, and the routes were the same as far as the bottom of Surbiton Hill where the 418 turned right through Surbiton and the 406 went straight ahead up the hill, the two meeting again at the top. I blame the SM, so used was I to turning right with an SM on the weekday 418 that I did the same on a Sunday.

Realising reasonably quickly (for me anyway) my mistake I pulled up at the first bus stop to think it through, where this lady passenger came to me and enquired was there a change of route or was I lost. Both questions were answered in the negative, the second I supplemented by adding that I knew I shouldn't be there, but I was definitely not lost. We then continued and joined the correct route at the top of Surbiton Hill. There were no stops on the 406 up Surbiton Hill so I didn't miss anyone, just lost about five minutes.

There were occasions when there was no work for me at Leatherhead and I could be loaned to Reigate garage where they were very short of crews, on the pretext that I would be used on the same route as operated by Leatherhead i.e., 406. Also sometimes I managed to get this on an overtime basis.

The new acquisition of a house was severely draining my resources. I arrived about 10.00 on a Saturday after having used an RF as a ferry bus, only to find there was no work on the 406, but would I consider a job on a 414, they asked. I agreed because I didn't want them saying to Leatherhead that they didn't want me anymore. The only problem was although I had a good idea of the Croydon end, the Horsham end was to say the least, vague. No problem I was assured; it's easy, just follow the main road, then the signs to the town centre near Horsham. This was basically true except for the last bit. On the approach to the town centre I was totally lost and, on looking around, the conductor was nowhere to be seen. Banging on the window I attracted a passenger's attention and managed to get through to her that I was lost, which way do we go? I mouthed and gestured. This happened a couple of times amid loads of laughter from her and three friends, and when I finally got out of the bus in Horsham, she said it made her day and gave me a big kiss – stupid lovely woman. Oh! Nearly forgot, the vehicle was an RMC.

The following Sunday I agreed to escort some relatives to Heathrow and we chose to take the 727. The return trip however meant that I caught the last but one from Heathrow back to Tadworth and the coach duly arrived in the pouring rain about five minutes early, I was pleased to see that the driver was someone I knew.

"I'm glad you're here," he said as he switched off the engine, "you can keep an eye on things whilst I go and find us some tea. It won't matter if we are a bit late leaving, as the traffic is very light at this time of night and we've only three on board." He soon returned and had a few mouthfuls before trying to fire up the engine, which unfortunately had other ideas; or rather the battery did. The internal lights and the headlights which he had left on just dimmed to almost nothing. Turning everything off and trying a few minutes later didn't improve things either. "I'll find the inspector" he said disappearing into the rain again, who strange as it may seem, couldn't start the bus (an RP) either.

"I'll phone Windsor" he announced, "this is their patch." He explained to the passengers the problem, who luckily didn't seem too bothered as they were only going to Kingston and opted to try another route. We waited and waited, then the next service coach arrived and departed (remember it was an hourly service) then lo and behold what have we? A breakdown gang, who after a quick prod with the jump leads got us started and on our way, with the stout message, "Don't turn the f***ing thing off," as if we would. The over helpful inspector then announced that although the last coach of the day had departed some twenty minutes earlier, he didn't want us taking any shortcuts home and we must take the correct line of route. We argued saying it was stupid and nobody would be expecting us, but to no avail; he insisted.

So off we went at a terrific rate of knots on the very clear roads with Ron demonstrating some driving methods that had been kept away from me during my training days. What speed limit? I didn't see one, RPs can shift.

On approaching Stoneleigh railway bridge he announced that the inspector's parents weren't married when he was born and we went via the by-pass instead of through Ewell village. Likewise he then opted to go up Reigate Road at Ewell by-pass, instead of the longer route through Epsom town, saying he would drop me off at Tadworth then continue along the A217 to Reigate. We had gone about half a mile up Reigate Road when the RP ground to a halt.

"I believe we've run out of gas" he suggested as we walked around the coach. At least the rain had stopped a bit. Then in these early hours of the morning I heard the gentle call of an old lady at her front gate summoning her cat in. Walking up to her slowly so as not to frighten her, I told of our problem and asked if we might use her phone. She was a dear, rather like Mrs Wilberforce in the 1955 film 'The Lady Killers', not only did she let us use her phone, but she insisted she made us tea and produced some home made cake to match.

The engineers at Reigate weren't so pleased though, asking what were we doing up Reigate Road, Ron said stop the questions and just get out here with the fuel and also to bring the jump leads.

To their credit they arrived very quickly, and got it started with very little bother. I suppose the fact that we hadn't repeatedly tried to start it after it stopped meant that we had not dragged much air into the fuel system. We thanked the old lady profusely and departed into the night. Apparently Ron was questioned about the whole affair the next day and the GTS agreed that in the circumstances, the Heathrow inspector was a bit stupid in his orders to go via line of route.

The next mad hat thing I agreed to was again because of no work on the 406 at Reigate. Huge problems with air travel at Gatwick Airport meant that passenger loadings were high on the 727 express coach route to Heathrow and Luton, and as a result extra vehicles could be useful. Muggins – me – said he knew the route from Gatwick Airport to Heathrow only.

The offer was taken up, a good RF was provided and off I went empty to Gatwick where I duly put up Heathrow on the front.

With a full load of passengers and luggage we set off almost non-stop to Heathrow. Arriving at Heathrow the chaos was as bad there as at Gatwick.

As the passengers were disembarking the inspector asked what was I up to. I told him of the agreement made at Reigate as I didn't know the route beyond Heathrow.

"What if I came with you as a pilot," he said, "would you take it to St Albans? There you could have a meal break, and whilst you were having it

I could get a local man to take it to Luton Airport and back." How could I refuse all these poor people standing in the rain, stranded in a strange country? It had happened to me some months earlier when I was in Poitiers in France, when the wonderful French rail workers decided to call a strike with about one hour's notice. By the way, Americans would try to pass a quarter dollar for a ten pence piece; these I would accept as actually they were worth about twenty pence, big money in them days!

"Load 'em on again. Which way?" "And by the way what is this place called?" I kept asking along the way. At St Albans I was relieved and went to the canteen for some eats.

Time to find my stead I thought after some considerable while, and look for my guide for the return. "Oh!, he's been gone a long time, probably home in Bedford by now," said the man in the office. The journey back was definitely not to route; there were certain landmarks we didn't pass on the way up. Telling the tale back at Reigate there was no pity. "Well you got here, and all that extra overtime, stop whingeing."

Generally I found SMs pleasant to drive; unlike the RF they were fitted with power steering and some had plenty of go in them. Their only real problem was that some had non existent front shock absorbers causing them to leap about when going over 30mph. The first time it happened to me, I was doing about 40mph on the dual carriageway approaching Tolworth station, and quite frankly it frightened the hell out of me. This feature became a good speed restricting device.

"Take one to Epsom," said the Inspector of the day, "Go round the Clock Tower and return on the 418." Out to the yard I went, found the allocated SM up by the shed end, set up "Private" and set off. Now everyone knows that to make a bus move entails putting your foot to the floor, and that is what I did. The only problem with this bus was that when I released my foot, the pedal stayed down, and we kept careering towards the row of buses parked on the slope. I don't know why, but I put both feet on the brake pedal pushing it right to the floor, causing the front wheels to lock up on the grease; but we stopped, and to stop the engine racing, I left it in gear, then immediately held in the engine stop button until it eventually stopped.

Reaching down to the stuck pedal, I pulled it up, then pushed it up and down again and it seemed OK. Not being an over trusting soul, I decided to get professional advice.

Entering the Engineers' office I was met by a fight going on with a driver complaining that his clean shirt had just been ruined by the dirt on the outside of a steering wheel. This dirt originates from a fitter with greasy hands and happens if he forgets to clean the wheel after his work.

The greeting to me was, "And what do you want?" My question was answered by the fitter who had followed me in. "I've just done a rota on that bus, there's nothing wrong with it."

"Just go and give it a quick road test," said the rather harassed Engineer.

To cover for the increasing failures, some interesting loans occurred. SM 483 still supports its yellow and blue 'Superbus' livery from Stevenage and was photographed in Epsom in June 1976. *Colin Fradd*

What a way to end your life! RT 2157 being used as a store at the rear of Leatherhead garage. To the right is what was RF 79 and now converted to an engineers' vehicle. *Roy Hobbs*

With a slamming of doors the fitter made a ceremonious exit, only to return five minutes later with a rather paler complexion saying, "He's right, it sticks down." In a foul mood he had gone full tilt toward the small round-about at the foot of Leatherhead bridge and when he took off his foot, guess what? – it kept going. They gave me another bus.

Another SM saga concerned one of the pair 111 and 112. These two had been lounging for some time out of use in the field opposite the garage await-ing engine repair. Eventually a rebuilt engine was fitted to SM 111, all the robbed bits were put back, and then I was given it for its first service run for many a month. (When vehicles are parked up for a while awaiting attention, it is normal for parts that are not available in the stores to be 'robbed' to allow other vehicles to be kept on the road).

It squeaked and groaned over every bump, probably due to the rust impregnated in the springs during its sojourn in the long grass. On our return from Kingston, by the time we had reached Epsom, the engine must have loosened up a bit, as the tickover got progressively faster, to such a degree that a different driving technique from normal was required.

SMs had a gear interlock fitted to both doors; when either was open, as at a bus stop, the bus idled in neutral gear. But with a fast tick-over, and even with the footbrake pushed firmly down, when the doors closed and it took up the selected pull away gear (usually 2nd) it leapt forward at quite an alarm-ing rate. This usually resulted in remarks from standing passengers about a rotten driver. The way to get over this was to select 4th first. This gave a slippy take up and had the effect of slowing down the engine to a very slightly more manageable speed. Then quickly select the pulling away gear, but don't use 1st, or the bus would rock even more violently back and forth. Actually, in a lot of cases SMs would quite happily pull away in 3rd on the flat. On arrival at Leatherhead SM 111 was subbed. The next day I had that SM again; the tick-over speed had been attended to, but not the squeaks.

Not all the poor rides could be blamed on the vehicle; some were driver created and I did my share.

The centre doors on ANs were controlled from a position on the gear switch. To open the door meant pushing the lever furthest to the left and then pushing it forward. To accelerate passenger disembarkation, the driv-ing technique adopted was to flick the gear lever into this doors open position just before coming to rest, knowing full well that the speed sensing system would not allow the doors to open until the vehicle was stationary. One day when using such a method I failed to push the lever far enough to the left before pushing it forward. 1st gear is up the channel before 'doors'. The result was instant first gear. Lucky we weren't going very fast otherwise everyone would have exited by the front doors.

One batch of ANs had their own in-built design problems, and Guildford's AN 101 I awarded 'Crap Bus of the Year 1973'. This bus was part of a batch fitted with Metro-Cammel bodies and had a very uncomfortable cab layout, necessitating you to lean forward a lot to operate your ticket machine. One evening I took over this vehicle to find the steering was heavy, was groaning on every turn and to cap it all whilst in the traffic at Merrow, the throttle pedal fell to the floor meaning I couldn't move the bus except on tickover. Having crept to the next bus bay, my trusted torch came into use yet again. By crawling about the floor I soon diagnosed the problem. The pedal was pivoted about the floor bracket by a steel pin. This pin had come out of the housing and allowed the pedal to drop out. At each end the pin had two small vacant drillings. Where were the small split pins, I asked myself.

One night a Leatherhead dual door AN made me ask myself a serious question – "what the **** was that?" I said to myself, as I was being bombarded by various components of the bus, just after applying the handbrake. The handbrake assembly consists of the operating stalk, a return spring, and a washer, all held on the valve operating shaft by a small screw. If this screw comes undone all the parts are catapulted away by the spring. Unfortunately in this condition there is nothing to hold the handbrake in the 'park' position. This little escapade required me to wedge the bus hard against a curb whilst yet again crawling on the cab floor with my torch to find the bits. If it had been a bus with manual transmission I could have turned off the engine and left it in gear to hold the bus stationary, but with a fluid flywheel that principle wouldn't work as there is no lock up between engine and wheels in that condition. These things always happened in the dark when you're running a bit late. Yet again that small screwdriver came in useful.

I thought I had a gear problem one Sunday evening when driving an MB across Epsom Downs, as the gears kept dropping out then returning. It was an excessive side wind that was strong enough to blow the centre doors open just enough for the gear interlock to operate, and that gives neutral.

Some of my frights were partially self-induced, and the next one I suppose I had a hand in – I thought the bus was on fire.

Again on a Sunday evening on the 406 but this time with an SM, where due to heavy traffic on the inward journey I had left Redhill about ten minutes down, and being a conscientious type had tried to make up time.

The first hurdle was to get this not over-willing machine up Reigate Hill. Usually if you got a good run at it, an SM would just about make it in 3rd, but not this one, so it was flat out in 2nd. Then while letting it roll down the hill towards Kingswood, when I looked in the mirror, panic; there were flames coming from the exhaust. But after a sharp pull up in the approaching bus bay, I could see no fire in the engine, so I continued rather gingerly for a while. Then as I turned into Ewell village just before Mongers Lane, I was awakened by the blue flashing lights of a police car, which shot past me and then pulled me over. My first thought was that the flames had returned and he's warning me of that, but no he was more interested in the lack of an offside rear light and asked if I knew about it. No – but it returned after a heavy clout. Back at the garage I spoke to a fitter who said the flames were the coke burning off from the hammering I gave it up the hill, probably did it some good. The light problem I wrote on the defect sign-off sheet, but of course it was still on and OK when we got back.

The next fright was definitely my fault and came when descending the 1 in 10 Hawks Hill in an AN just before Leatherhead garage. Suddenly the flag dropped and the gears assumed the neutral position – no brakes I thought, and Oh merde, as the appropriate words in my French dictionary suddenly returned to mind. What had happened was that I had inadvertently switched off the bus. Like many drivers, I used to hang my cash bag which contained all my bits around the push buttons on the control panel, which is conveniently placed down on the left side. As I was finishing at the garage I was dumping my personal fare chart (with my own marked out sections on it) in the bag, and in doing so, had accidentally knocked in the master push button switch and effectively turned off part of the bus. Actually I still had brakes, and maybe also soiled underpants!

The route to Boxhill, or rather the RF I took up there, exhibited a peculiar phenomenon. Turning right at the triangle into Boxhill Road necessitated reversing back and having a second bite at it. Never noticed that before, I thought; well perhaps I set it up wrong, it's a bit tight there.

On the return journey there was no problem. Strange because it's about a 140 degree turn, plenty of left lock, but I noticed it was accompanied by a rubbing sound. Examination showed that the inside of the left tyre had been rubbing on the inside of the mudguard. This I reported on the vehicle defect sheet, and was later told it was caused by whoever fitted the tie rods to the steering rack not setting them to equal distance on each side. To go straight ahead the steering wheel would need to be off centre to compensate, but you wouldn't know this when driving normally. Only a tight corner would show it up, with an over amount of left lock but hardly any on the right, and that accounted for my right turn problem. It wasn't me after all, that time.

RFs were beginning to show their age and some of the maintenance methods didn't help either. Late afternoon, taking over a 462 outside LH garage, the retiring driver said it had boiled earlier, he had topped her up, but now she was boiling again.

Right Some of the roads we traversed were quite narrow. Here we see AN 35 on the narrow section past Mickleham church in spring 1977. Often on a Sunday mid-day this section was difficult to navigate because of cars parked outside the pub; the white building to the rear of the bus. *R. Hobbs*

Inspecting the level I decided it needed more; maybe there was an airlock. Two cans later and we were on our way to Addlestone, but by Cobham we were boiling again. Pulling into Addlestone garage forecourt amongst the steam, I was spotted by a friendly fitter who said he would look at it whilst I had my meal break. The exotic meal I was enjoying from the canteen was interrupted by his words, "The head was loose and jumping about all over the place and the oil level is quite a bit high." So that's where all the water went – into the sump. Anyway by now the day was cooling a bit and the traffic was getting lighter. "I've informed Leatherhead, so they will have a changeover for you," he said.

Arriving at Leatherhead no replacement could be seen and everyone denied being told from Addlestone of a problem. "Well you know of it now" I said. "Oh she'll be all right, she's been like that for days, it's a quiet route and the evening is quite cool now." I didn't really relish the thought of breaking down somewhere in the middle of nowhere on that lonely dark 462 road to Weybridge Hospital, which was where the next one went to.

Therefore my message became: no new bus, me go nowhere. It didn't take long to find one, an ex Green Line refurbished vehicle with four headlights, just right for the un-lit roads between Fetcham then through Stoke d'Abernon and on to Cobham.

PASSENGERS

ANs can give pleasure, or rather some of the passengers can. One AN ride will always stick in my mind as it provided one of the best bits of entertainment ever.

The last 408 from Guildford to Leatherhead normally ran empty past Horsley. Plodding along the A246 half asleep, I was quickly awakened by the vision from the upper deck in the periscope mirror. A couple were enacting a scene from Kama Sutra. Cleaning the mirror improved the quality slightly but not sufficient to see what page they were on. This road is not lit, a bit narrow and twisty in places, parts have no footpath and bushes hang over the road. It was difficult to divide my concentration.

Arriving on the forecourt at Leatherhead amongst the buses waiting to be fuelled, the man came down first. "You'll have to come through the front doors, there seems a problem with the centre ones," I said, because I wanted to see the pretty maiden close up. Passing me with "Goodnight Mate," he went into the darkness. His lady love followed a few paces behind and wished me goodnight also. "Goodnight and thank you," I said as she passed. She stopped and said "Thank you for what?" "For the entertainment," I said, pointing to the periscope mirror. "I can see all that goes on up there." Emitting a scream of "Oh no," she leapt from the bus and ran off into the night dragging her partner with her.

The younger generation need some special mention. An afternoon trip from Croydon collects hoardes of the female gender at Carshalton 'Windsor

Castle'. Some had free passes, some had to pay. One such fare payer was taking her time in finding her money, so I just sat there gazing into space as she fiddled with her purse. The gaze tuned into the nearside mirror to a view of objects being dropped from the upper deck to the waiting queue below. I had been warned of this practice. The objects were of course the free passes of the girls already on the bus, and would be re-used by the supposed fare paying girls yet to board. "So, you want to play silly buggers with Rod do you?" "Sorry, we're full up," I shouted, closing the doors at the earliest opportunity, and it looked that way too, but only because it took a lot of persuading to get those yacking females to move down the bus.

Next morning should be fun, I thought; those free passes are in the wrong hands. I reported the incident to the garage who apparently put a Jumper on the trip they usually took in the morning. I didn't hear the outcome.

Between West Croydon and Wallington Green the 408/470 shared the route with the 403 group, and at West Croydon it was common practice for passengers to board whichever bus left first.

This meant them waiting at the 403 stop, just to the rear of the 408/470 terminating stop, and if the 403 came first they took that; if not, they waited for you to start the engine and got on yours. Unless you returned to your bus early and started your engine, your departure from there could be delayed by this sudden influx of passengers. What I did, and I suppose it was a bit mean – but I did it to keep to departure time – was shut the doors, let the bus roll down the slope then start it on the move.

Boxhill was connected to Leatherhead via two routes. The 416 went via Headley and the RAF Hospital, the 422 via the slightly shorter route via Tot Hill. Both were busy mid-morning with shoppers.

"14p, please" was the usual request. The one 13p raised the question, "Where are you going, Madam?" "To the town of course, why?" "I'm sorry but it's 14p to the town," "No it's not, it's 13, I always pay 13." Being a coward with women, I decided I needed reinforcements, even if it meant from women, but this time I considered I was on a winner.

Leaning from the cab of the RF, I attracted the attention of the woman in the first seat. "How much to Leatherhead?" I asked. "14p" came the reply – soon to be supported by others. "Well this lady insists it's 13," I said."Don't let that scheming bitch get away with that," came the unanimous response from half of the bus. "She's always up to something." Obviously, I thought, she's well known to the small tight knit community of Boxhill. The 14p was paid and a quiet ride to Leatherhead ensued.

One section of the crazy fare structure related to dogs, which were carried at half the adult fare everywhere, including the parts under GLC ticket rules. Which meant between Kingston and Tolworth, dogs paid 4p on a London Country bus, but only 3p on a red one, i.e. the child's fare for that journey. This little difference did cause some disagreements at times. Sometimes however, I deliberately didn't notice the dog.

Carshalton also boasted a hostel for visiting foreign students, and during their stay, Croydon was a natural haunt for them. "6 pence please" was the request from the first in the queue. "Where are you going?" I asked, and "how old are you?" "French," came the reply accompanied by a smile, pretending he didn't understand my question. "Ou allez-vous et quel age avez-vous?" I said in my best French for a long time. His smile withered as he replied, "J'ai seize ans et je vais a Croydon, (I'm sixteen). "Alors, vous devez payer douze pence si vous plait," (then you must pay twelve pence please) finished the discussion. Luckily he passed the message to his group and they all paid up the same. When about eighteen I had a very pretty French pen friend, and during our actual meetings I did pick up some other useful words from her, apart from "je t'aime."

The younger generation and Carshalton came again into the news. Thursday night was their youth club evening. Where was the regular driver that evening, was I set up? Anyway the patrons boarding in Carshalton were around the 14 year mark, shouting, pushing and doing all the same things we have all done in our youth.

"Arf ter Sutton," said the next youth, considerably bigger built but obviously of similar age to the rest. "You with them?" "Yer, why?" "How would you like a free ride home?" I asked "Yer". His face lit up. "But, in return you will have to keep all that lot quiet and under control, OK you know what I mean?" "Yer." He then steamed off down the bus shouting, "Sit down and shurrup you lot." They did.

The next day the Garage Traffic Superintendent asked me how I got on with those unrulies. When I told him what I did he remarked, "You're a case, you really are," and just walked away shaking his head.

Then there was this very well spoken lady in Cheam, with a character rather like Margot in the TV series 'The Good Life'.

"Epsom, driver – single, how much?" "Oh dear, I don't seem to have enough, will a cheque do?" "No madam, I'm afraid we aren't allowed to take them." "Well my man if they are good enough for shops they should be good enough for you," and she began writing. I repeated my message calmly, to which she said, "If that's how you feel," then turned around as about to leave and miraculously found an amount of loose change which she dumped on the tray. Moving up the bus she uttered some adjectives not fitting a lady with such a well bred Surrey accent. So yet again I was in trouble with the Garage Traffic Superintendent.

"Do you remember yesterday a well spoken lady objecting because you refused a cheque?" "Yes, that was me." "Good, it was you; I checked during her phone call, but I know sometimes you lot swap duties," he said. 'So, were you abusive as she claimed?" "No." "That's good because I already told her that I knew the driver and that I didn't believe he would behave in that fashion. I then reinforced your statement that all bus fares had to be paid in cash. Do you know Rod, she hung up?"

Dogs, I love, but some don't like buses, or is it they are just not used to them? A lady and her big doggie boarded in Epsom town bound for Epsom Common, where she got off. From what I could see in the mirror of the dual door AN, all was clear of the centre doors.

Shouts of "Not yet, not yet" came from the bus. I stopped, switched off and walked toward the centre doors. The big doggie was frightened of the big drop to the pavement and refused to move. The lady was outside the bus holding the other end of the lead, which was neatly threaded through the door rubber to the dog on the inside. Leads being thin, will allow the inter-lock to assume that the doors are safely closed and gears will be available. Without starting up the bus, I then opened the doors on the local emergency tap, and with a big push managed to persuade him to jump.

One of the duties meant you had the same bus all day and it necessitated a special long card to hold all the information. It started with the once a day direct 416 from Tadworth to Esher, and the lady who boarded in Walton on the Hill said, "See you later" as she got off in Esher. What does she mean I wondered, she's not trying to pick me up I hope!

The RF and I did a return to Boxhill on the 416, and after that a rounder on the 422; then we had a meal break, and after a couple of shorts to Fetcham on the 462, returned to Esher for the last leg to Tadworth. There was that lady, returning to Walton on the Hill, obviously a regular who knew the duty pattern. This duty was fine, provided you had a decent bus.

Ex Green Line RF 54 with its twin headlights made driving at night on the unlit roads much easier than with the non-refurbished variety. It is approaching Box Hill in September 1977 opposite the 'Hand in Hand' public house. *Colin Fradd*

RF 625 in West Street, Epsom, on the 419 bound for Langley Vale in March 1974. The total journey time from end to end was 23 minutes, and right from the introduction of the service it always supported 'lazy' blinds. The shortest route from LH was the 481 between Epsom and the Wells Estate. This had a running time of only nine minutes in each direction, which from the driver's point of view could be a bore, particularly on a Saturday when you did about six 'rounders' in succession. *Colin Fradd*

THE FINAL DAY IS NIGH

The day finally came along with that long awaited phone call. I had been head hunted by an audio research company, which had made me an offer too good to resist.

Asking at the office for the necessary notice to quit form was not very pleasant, as I had been very happy doing my little fill-in job for the last seven months; and in a way was regretting leaving. However, this new position offered a reasonable increase in income and job opportunities and I would be a fool to refuse.

In actuality, working on the buses I had earned more than I had when working at my earlier research job. This peeved me a bit; it took me years hard slogging at college and night school to get the knowledge necessary to perform that job, and there was I, virtually walking in off the street and earning £2,200 a year against my previous £1,900. However, this extra £300 allowed me to get a £900 bigger mortgage.

I was very dubious of what I saw during the last week of my employment at Leatherhead.

There was this strange looking new single-deck bus with a body that extended over the wheel arches, looking as if the chassis was too narrow and, from the side, with sliding windows it looked a bit like a GS without the nose.

Jumping in the cab I noticed it had a gear lever and three pedals; manual gearbox I decided, now that will be fun. Any driver passed within the last three years would, like me, have an 'automatic only' licence and need to be re-tested, and many of those old timers who had 'all types' seemed to be unable to master a semi, so what would they make of this? It was a BL – the 8ft wide version of the 7ft 6in wide BN soon to be introduced at Leatherhead, initially on the 416/422 to Boxhill where it was considered that the forth-coming Nationals would be too wide – the RF's days were numbered and in fact to a lesser degree so were the SMs.

My last day was upon me. I signed on feeling quite subdued, did a complete rounder on the 418 and for the second half, just a Kingston and back finishing about 19.30. The last vehicle I drove was SM 107, which coincidentally was the very same vehicle I first drove in service on my own.

So I said a few quick good-byes to the office staff and got on my old Lambretta model D and crawled off via the 422 route to home.

And that ended my bus driving days.

Or did it?

I'M BACK

It was six years since I had taken that wonderful position offered to me when working on the buses previously, but all good things come to an end and redundancy was on the horizon yet again. I'll work for myself, I decided. I'll use some of the redundancy money to buy some test equipment and set myself up as an engineer specialising in the repair of expensive hi-fi equipment. I already had some good contacts. The only problem was it would take a while to get going and get enough money coming in. Back to the buses I thought; that will give me the extra support for a while.

We were by now well settled into our Tadworth house and involved in local activities. One such was to record my friend's daughter's wedding at a local church. The verger who greeted me at the door seemed to know me very well, but I couldn't immediately place the face – his black robes didn't help either, then the voice again, yes it was – John the GTS from LH doing his bit for the community. I apologised for not instantly recognising him but I had been away from bus work for over five years. It transpired we only lived about a mile apart. Anyway, I must have made a mark; he remembered me well and after the ceremony he asked what was I doing in life. I told of my near future not too good job prospects. "Come back to the buses for a while," he said, "I'll take you back." So there it was.

Being in his office on that Monday morning four weeks later I didn't have the same anxiety as six years previously. I was introduced to another gent there as a man who repairs radios. The gent I recognised as the GTS from Reigate (RG) who said I ought to go to RG as it was closer to my home, and did I do repairs in my spare time? He had one needing attention. Also he had a friend with a radio shop and could get me some work (probably take 10% though). Now I had not told either of them my real reason for coming back. In the end I stayed at LH. There were no arithmetic tests or story writings on this occasion, only the appearance of a not very happy and decidedly offish driving assessor.

Although knowing of my past bus driving experience, when on the RT out in the yard, he insisted on going through all the operating procedures for a pre-selector and then proceeded to drive it for about two miles without uttering a word! Finally at Givons Grove roundabout on the 470 route he stopped and I took over, went along the main A24 to Burford Bridge, around the roundabout and back to LH, not one of my best demonstrations by a long chalk. At the end he accused me of using the operating pedal like a clutch.

This can be the effect if you put on the gas a bit soon and also let the operating pedal up slowly. All vehicles are different and really I didn't have time to realise this one's characteristics. In fact I probably only changed gear about five times, I was just trying to get a smooth change. Anyway he accepted my explanation (just). Later in the office they said he was always a bit sour and one should always ask him about his bowls – his pastime, which usually cheered him up. They were right.

LEARNING AGAIN

During my six years absence much had changed. All the crew work had gone and obviously all the RMCs and RTs too. Some of the dual door ANs had been replaced by the single door variety, and the RFs and SMs had been replaced by a mixture of Leyland Nationals SNB, ex SNCs and the later "B" series SNBs. For the Boxhill route, Nationals were considered too large so there was a small allocation of BNs. These little machines had manual transmission which my still valid 'any type of automatic PSV' licence didn't cover, so it was off to the training school again for another PSV test.

Monday morning at 8.30 sharp in the LH canteen I met my instructor. Pete like the instructor on my earlier employ was a temporary man, and his parent garage was Guildford (GF), that place I could never find in the dark six years previously. My buddy in crime was to be Derek, and his previous job was a saucepan salesman. Derek had also driven buses before but like me, didn't have a manual licence. Pete very quickly showed me the controls of the bus and because he had started the previous week, left it to Derek to show me how.

The first "how" turned out to be how to have an argument with a bread van. The back roads from Horsley to Guildford are not very wide, certainly not enough for a BN and a bread van when travelling at speed in opposite directions. I considered it a bit tight and thought a reduction in speed of both vehicles would be advisable. But I was alone in this and both the bread van and BN continued at their same paces. Even Pete kept quiet, quiet that was until the inevitable happened – we scraped. Luckily not too hard, the only damage to the bus being the partial removal of the rear emergency door hinges, but the door stayed in place. Afterwards we went slower and Pete paid more attention. Being Pete's home garage we easily found GF and had tea and 'watered the horses' there. Seeing the tight restrictions on the approaches to the garage I was glad I didn't find it on that dark night six years previously. Derek then drove us sedately to Merrow, where I took over, my first time at the wheel of a BN.

It had a stiff gear stick, a heavy clutch and no power steering but in its favour plenty of engine power. I took it a bit slowly along the dual carriageway of the A246, with Derek saying didn't I know that there were five forward gears and that I was still in 4th. I replied quite sternly that I am getting familiar with the bus and will go faster when I think fit.

I detected that Pete and Derek looked at each other, and Derek must have felt a bit guilty, as he reminded me that hitting bread vans was his domain.

BN training was usually done locally around Sutton and Croydon with the occasional visit to Guildford and very occasionally the interesting roads (well to me anyway) in the area bounding Newdigate, Leigh, Betchworth and Beare Green. Interesting because although I lived not far away, I rarely got to go down that way, and often wondered where they led to. Provided the suggestions were sensible, most instructors were quite open to ideas of where to go for the day, as they were often lost for ones of their own. Perhaps the furthest we got to was Pete's friend's house in Edenbridge; we had this special project to move a large wardrobe from there to a location in Shalford. To get this item of furniture on the bus meant us partially dismantling it and then rebuilding it later. The route took us over roads that were unknown to us and were very narrow in places, so the trip was very instructive and certainly not in vain.

There were three very important things to remember about BNs. Reverse was in a similar position to 2nd, but for reverse, a little bit of extra pressure was required down on the stick, and on some vehicles the reverse interlock was a bit weak, so you could easily select reverse instead of 2nd when stationary. If you got it wrong on the move, the noise of a complaining gearbox gave the game away! Secondly, there was something strange about the tyres fitted as they could slide very easily on a wet surface. At times you could get wheel spin on pull away if you gave it too much gas. And thirdly (but there were probably a lot more), the BN didn't have power steering and some examples needed a bit of pulling to get round and could catch you out sometimes. The BN was so different to any other class of bus, and to me it was a pleasure to drive if only because it so was different.

Getting to LH some mornings for the training trips could be a problem as we only had one car, and the Lambretta had some serious problems making it unusable. However, my wife also worked in Leatherhead and some days she would go in a bit early and drop me off at LH. The getting home was usually achieved by asking Pete if we could go back past my house. The route from there to Leatherhead was a bus route (416) with some quite narrow roads, so good practice for Derek. This door to door service usually meant that I bought the round of tea in the last canteen stop, which was generally Godstone or Reigate. I always got this request in early in the day so Pete could plan the routes.

Above right Apart from the BNs, the other type of training vehicles with manual gearboxes were these ex-Ribble Leyland PD3s, and were nicknamed Yellow Perils". Here is one photographed on the forecourt of Dorking Bus Garage. If you passed out on one of these, you received an "all types PSV" licence. *Roy Hobbs*

Right AN 126 when brand new, outside Leatherhead garage, about to embark on a journey to West Croydon. *Roy Hobbs*

WHAT A DAY! – THE TEST

The day of the test, Monday 14th May 1979, arrived very quickly, and like that of six years earlier the day was sunny. This time we were to meet the examiner (and what a happy individual!) in the canteen of Thornton Heath (TH) London Transport garage.

Derek chose to go first and drove very well (no bread vans today). We toured the roads around Croydon and the Roundshaw Estate, where Derek was directed to stop so that I could take over. He was also directed (or should I say shouted at), to "make the bus safe." Derek just sat and looked rather puzzled by the command; the bus was in neutral, the hand brake on. He looked at the curb, then to the offside, then down the bus to me – I shrugged my shoulders, the bus appeared to be parked safely.

"Turn it off," shouted the examiner. Derek pulled the stop lever under the driver's seat, but like a lot of BNs, it wouldn't stop. This fact Derek reported, only to be greeted by, "Well stall the f***ing thing," which he did.

I then took over with 'Happy' shouting instructions from his seat halfway down the bus. At the traffic lights in Coulsdon for no apparent reason the engine stalled, then again at the pedestrian lights by Star Lane. Of course it goes without saying this was noticed by the examiner and questions were raised. "What's the matter with you, don't you know to push the clutch down when you stop?"

Pete then informed him the bus had a tendency to stall when hot – more four letter words from him. We went towards Caterham, then up the steep hill and the sharp curve past Woldingham station. Along the road at the top I was directed to the left – left, I thought, where are we going? I am sure that after these few houses this road becomes single track. Oh well, perhaps I'm wrong; it's been a long time since I've come this way, maybe there's an estate here now.

This time however I was right, very soon the bushes were rubbing on the side of the bus, then a sharp corner and in front a hill with about a one in six gradient. It was at about this point that I became aware of the examiner standing alongside me. He then said in a slightly more amicable tone, "Are you all right driver? I got the directions slightly wrong in the village back there." Yes, I thought, I bet you brought me down here just for a laugh. By now we were getting slower and slower and already in 2nd gear, this is it I decided – 1st on the move – could be fun. With it nearly at stall I double declutched into 1st – beautiful I thought, so did he. "No need for that again," he said. My memory says that the lane comes out on the Limpsfield Road just a bit south of Chelsham garage.

Back at TH we both answered our Highway Code questions well and both passed, a good job because while Pete, Derek and myself were celebrating with Pete buying us all a cup of tea, the examiner came and asked us for a push in his van as the battery was flat. Now I wonder what the answer would have been if we had failed?

Advert bus AN 50 running from GF on a 408A around the Merrow loop. *Author*

London Transport maintained a presence in Leatherhead with Route 71, which terminated in the garage forecourt. *Colin Fradd*

The licence given when passing on a BN has a restriction to a length of 27 feet 6 inches, and of course single deck. This was to stop drivers going to other employment and driving coaches, which were normally longer.

To add to the celebration, Peter the instructor said he would drive us home. At Wallington Green lights the engine stalled. Our mutual applause soon stopped when it refused to turn over; it was absolutely dead, and by doing a few quick checks like putting on the headlights and operating the starter, the fact that the lights didn't go dim gave us the assurance that the battery was not flat and that the fault lay in the starter circuit. Unfortunately the road is flat at that point so there was no question of bump starting it.

Phoning the nearest garage, Chelsham, brought a negative response; they refused to come out. Luckily there was a small bakery close by that sold some rather nice sausage rolls and tea, so we were well catered for. Leatherhead eventually arrived an hour and a half later, by which time we had succeeded in causing quite a traffic jam, because we were blocking one lane on the approach to the lights.

The yellow breakdown tender was RF 79, which had been converted to an engineer's vehicle, and was driven by a fitter who was convinced that we had flattened the battery by the continual starting on the test. "Why then" I asked, "did the headlights not dim when we pushed the starter button?" He ignored this question from a mere bus driver and instead unrolled the battery jump leads and proceeded to connect them between the two vehicles. Of course when he tried again the response was no different.

"So, clever Dick what do you reckon now?" he asked me. I could have sulked and said nothing, but I did rather want to get home and didn't fancy being towed all the way.

"My Mini had the same fault when the brushes in the starter motor got a bit low."

"And how did you cure the Mini?"

"I hit the starter with a hammer."

One hard clout with this special "fix-it all" tool and we were back in business. Peter had the instruction from us "no stalling, or else".

Arriving back at Leatherhead the bus was immediately taken from us and put into service!

Right Two views of BNs. From the first batch is BN 46 at Netherne Hospital, and below from the second batch is BN 67 which according to the blind display will or has been doing the 419 shorts between Epsom and Brettgrave, which only ran on Thursdays and Sundays. The slight difference between the two batches in front windscreen and blind aperture mounting arrangements can be seen. Behind is an RN, ex Barton Transport. These vehicles had seats arranged 3 one side of the aisle and 2 the other and were mainly used on the 418 and school duties. Alongside is AN 35. *Colin Fradd/R. Hobbs*

A QUICK BRUSH UP, THAT'S ALL

Because of my previous experience, type training was rushed through with only a short trip on a single door AN and then one day with another novice on an SNC proper from RG. That was quite an interesting day as we toured all the narrow roads around Newdigate, Rusper and Leigh just like some of our BN training routes, which according to Pete were actual bus routes. All the time though we quite expected it to fail, as the low oil pressure warning light was continuously on. We had brought it to the attention of a fitter at Reigate before we left but he said it had sufficient oil in the sump and it was OK to take it. This time he was either right or we were lucky.

The training in fare collection consisted of a day at Reigate; no more going out acting as a conductor, there weren't any, and then of me being accompanied by an instructor on a service duty with me driving, taking the fares and route familiarisation all in one go! This lasted for two days.

The first morning was on my old route, the 406, with an SNB. No-one had said the route had changed, it no longer went down Surbiton Hill. But that morning it did. The instructor was reading a newspaper and just assumed I knew where to go. There were also changes on the approach to Croydon, and on the 408, the Effingham Woodlands Road turn had been extended about a mile further, to Effingham 'Sir Douglas Haig', a pub. The 418, 419 and 481 were moulded into the 476, 478 and 479 group, which generally started in Kingston, with the 476 going via Longmead Estate on the approach to Epsom, after which it went to Langley Vale (ex 419) and the others to Bookham; the 479 doing a double run via The Wells (ex 481). There were a few school specials, but more on those later.

So, two days later and I was on my own again, but just like old times I managed not to get on the rota but did 'instructions' and any other odd job that came along. One odd job included going as a pilot with a new driver who was unsure of the route. He was already in the seat of the 'B' series SNB outside the garage and ready to go when I joined him; the day was a scorcher. After taking the fares in Ashtead he said he couldn't take the bus any further unless he had a breather outside the bus as the cab was stifling, he couldn't turn off the heaters – true it was like an oven in there. National heaters were always a mystery. Some of the early 'A' series had automatic control, some had the automatic modified with an over-ride toggle switch; generally it was fiddle with everything until you achieved your requirement. 'Bs' had none of this as they had no pod on the roof. What no-one told you, and there was no mention of it in the vehicle instruction leaflet, was that to turn off the heaters you merely turned off the water flow by a stopcock in the cabinet under the front nearside windscreen. Simple when you knew.

FULLY AUTOMATIC, A SMOOTHER RIDE

Three of the semi-automatic buses in the London Country fleet had been converted to fully automatic transmission and at Leatherhead our AN 124 (the first of the single door variety) was so treated. Basically the gates on the gear selector were modified to have reverse, automatic and hold positions only. The bus still retained its five speed gearbox. In Automatic position, the pull away gear was what one would normally use on a semi-automatic bus – that is, 2nd.

If for any reason you wanted to start in 1st, then you selected hold. Hold also inhibited up-changes; if you wanted to go faster before it changed up you selected Hold and when you wanted it to change, you moved the lever either out of Hold and back again or from Hold to Automatic. In Automatic there was only one up-change speed point for each gear, i.e., it did not change dependent on the throttle load position like some of the systems being fitted to other fleets.

The biggest annoyance of this fixed speed up-change was when you wanted to drive slowly, it would remain in 4th and not go into 5th at a low speed. The only way to get it to change up was to go faster, get it to change up then slow down slightly. All this knowledge I took in and used later in my career when working on the electronic side of vehicle transmission design. Included in the automatic fitment was a throttle dip. This takes the throttle off during up-changes.

On AN 124, the timing of gear release and throttle dip had been well chosen and it gave a very smooth ride. At one time I thought the pump had been modified as the acceleration appeared better than a normal semi. I then decided it was probably because of the quick change it was achieving, and this theory led me to experiment with my gear changing. Then one day I spied the bus being looked at by my friendly fitter, who explained it was fitted with 'quick dump valves' which almost eliminated the hanging on of gears.

I then decided what was needed on a five speed semi was to keep the throttle on just a very little after moving the shift to neutral, but not as long as on the RMCs. If you left it too long engine flair would occur because you were then in neutral. Then a quick flip of the lever to the higher gear followed by the accelerator, which in fact was almost an up and down operation. And because on a five speed gearbox the ratios were very close, it was not necessary to let the revs drop to nearly tickover before selecting the next gear, so an almost instant next gear selection could be used.

This technique I practised and got some very smooth changes and faster rides; it also gave me great satisfaction. The taught method of waiting for the revs to drop very low was only really applicable to the wider ratio four speed gearbox.

LIFE'S NEVER BORING
There were several school specials, some advertised in the public timetable while others were contracted with individual schools and always had a teacher as a guide.

One public run went from Stamford Green school situated off the normal bus route and in quite a nice residential location, to Langley Vale. After joining the main road, it went into Epsom town via the old 419 (by now 476), then around the back of the station, up Ashley Road via the normal 406 to the Downs then via Langley Vale Road (a non-bus route) to the Vale. The allocated vehicle was a BN and the journey was advertised as a 476.

An interesting note on the fare chart said that although after 16.00 hours, all children were to be charged at the child rate, and not the adult fare which started after that time.

The day I did the turn was a race day, and quite congested, as some race goers had begun to make an early getaway, but we managed to get through with no real problem. Being a normal race meeting and the last race not yet run, Ashley Road traffic was still in two directions.

Passing the gypsy caravans parked on the Downs in the fields close to Langley Vale Road, all the windows of the BN were forced to their widest, and whilst in the slow moving traffic, the children on my bus chanted "Go away gyppoes," at the gypsy children close by who were sitting outside their vans in the sun. "Shuttup" I shouted, as an equally strong return chorus began, "or you'll have us all lynched." I waited for missiles but they didn't materialise. I think we were lucky that the traffic suddenly moved and that there was a fence between us.

Some children are very strange and quite sweet. As the last little lad got off at Harding Road terminus in Langley Vale, he asked that as I was going back via Beaconsfield Road where he lived, could he stay on and be dropped off near the bottom, which I did. As the little chap got off he left a tip on the money tray. I did of course insist he took it back.

Actually the Langley Vale loop on the 476 was quite long with only two stops. The first was at the bottom of Rosebery Road, the next about 1000 yards away at the Harding Road terminus, which for a densely populated housing area was a bit far. This being my old home ground I often made an unofficial stop on the way in, halfway up Rosebery Road just before the turn into Harding Road outside the church, so that people who lived at the top of Rosebery Road could get off. This saved them walking back about 150 yards from where we had just come.

One private school special was accompanied by wonderful directions, which said: approach Sir Douglas Haig pub from Effingham traffic lights and take the second turning before the cross roads on the right, then left at the end then second left. The teacher will be waiting in the bus bay just as you rejoin the main road. Now how do you know its the second turning before until you've got to the cross roads? And in that particular case it turned out to be the same loop as the Haig turn on a normal 408. Of course I didn't know that so I missed the turn. The teacher saw me coming toward her on the other side of the road and started to panic and shout to me that I was going the wrong way.

"Calm down, stay there, I will turn round," I shouted, as I reversed the AN into the narrow street I should have come down, and then stopped alongside her. All it needed was a three or five point turn because of the parked cars, no problem. "I didn't know you could do that in a bus" she said. Remembering what I had witnessed a couple doing one night, I nearly replied that there's probably a lot of things you don't know of that can be done in a bus, but I thought better of it. Quite a pretty little thing when you got close.

The next day, Derby day, I was doing a late afternoon clean up instruction on the 406 with an SNB. After a really exciting meal I was instructed by the inspector at Kingston to do a run as far as Tadworth. At the Queen Adelaide on the Kingston Road a gentleman boarded in rather a huff complaining he had been waiting half an hour, and then proceeded to take a long time in finding his money. He didn't appreciate my question, which was why in that time could he not have got his money ready and save us further delay?

Tattenham Corner stop was as expected, with many revellers (some quite intoxicated) coming away from the funfair. They weren't very happy that we were only going to Tadworth, saying that they had already been waiting for over half an hour. "Can't you go further?" came the request, "we've got return tickets." "Well I can ask," I said. It didn't bother me I was on overtime anyway.

At Tadworth station I phoned the garage and reported the situation. "Take it through. Better to do that than have a load of aggressive drunks for the next one or for you to deal with now," came the answer. Cheers came as I wound up a blank ultimate and announced the good news. My intention was only to go as far as I had passengers. In fact the last one got off at Reffels Bridge, just short of Redhill, so I decided to go on to the station terminus and use the loo in the pub opposite.

Returning as an in service journey to Leatherhead garage seemed to please the next bunch on the Downs as the majority hailed from Ashtead. If I was on a commission for these journeys I would have done well on passenger satisfaction.

Then I did it again – got it wrong that is. For some while I had been doing regular covers on the 408 to Guildford. This morning I was on a 468, the only one which goes dead to, and starts from East Horsley Bishopsmead Parade, a road off the 408 route by Horsley Towers. It is scheduled for an AN but today I have a BN.

I'm quite happy at 7.45 in the morning: the sun is shining and I'm singing in time with the rattling of the bus. Just before the church at West Horsley, I think, what the hell am I doing here? I should have turned right about half a mile back. I had been so used to going along all the length of the main road on my way to Guildford. Spying a farm entrance on the right and ensuring there was nothing behind me I quickly did a reverse into the farm and headed back towards Horsley.

One of the scariest moments in my life concerned a National. I had been asked to take this vehicle over to Reigate and this I presumed was a normal stock move. I decided to go to Epsom on the A24 as far as Wilson's garage on the outskirts of Epsom, go right on to the old 419, then up over the Downs, then via the 406 to Reigate. All was going quite peacefully until the hill down into Langley Vale. Funny I thought as I touched the brakes to slow down, she's died, releasing the brakes she came back again. Panic then set in, the engine wasn't dying, the rear wheels were locking up on the barely wet road, the engine was just going back to tickover. Several times I gently applied the brakes with the same result. By now Langley Vale village was getting close and the bus was not slowing to a speed suitable for the corner past the garage and grocer's shop where vehicles were often parked outside. I was in two minds whether to crash the vehicle through the fence into the field, but declined and instead continued to hit the brakes. Luckily the road was clear and we made it. I was very wary for the rest of the journey, particularly down Reigate Hill. At Reigate, I warned an engineer to beware of the bus as the rear wheels keep locking up. His reply, "Yes Mate, I know, that's what you brought it over for," did kind of annoy me.

In later years I learned that this problem was a slight design fault which was exaggerated by certain brake shoe types.

Advertising on the sides of our buses had been really promoted and in the main was taken up by local estate agents. Instead of the old method of preparing the advertisement on a paper base, the modern technique was to print it on vinyl, which was then fixed to the side of the bus with some adhesive that also attacked the paint, so when the time came to remove the vinyl, it usually removed layers of paint also, resulting in bare patches of panelling being visible. In practice the advert was often left in place even though the contract had finished.

THE VEHICLES ARE ALL AGAINST ME

I believe vehicle problems are on the increase, I thought to myself, when one of my old favourite dual door ANs disgraced itself on a return trip from Croydon. On pulling away from Wallington Green traffic lights there was this almighty bang like a gun going off, followed by a sudden retardation of the bus. I managed to coast it so as not to cause too much obstruction at the junction. Walking to the rear I was greeted by pools of oil flowing from the engine.

The bang was the flywheel fuse plug leaving the flywheel at a terrific rate of knots and hitting the engine cover; the oil was previously contained within the flywheel. The garage was called with a message to ask the police to visit the scene with a quantity of sand to mop up the oil. Their comment on arrival was, "Not another one; there was one in the same spot three days ago." In fact it was exactly the same spot where we had broken down with the BN when returning from the test some weeks previously.

This occurrence must have made the garage a bit twitchy with flywheels. A few days later, the AN I took to an Effingham start had so much slip in the transmission you could basically flip the gear lever wherever you wanted and not feel the change and the engine revs stayed the same. At Effingham, I quickly phoned them, with the result that a fitter contingent was awaiting my arrival outside the garage with their flywheel filling kit. Unfortunately on checking the flywheel, the oil, was to the correct level.

The bus was subbed. I later learned that the main line air pressure was about 30lb psi instead of around 70. Pressure that low would cause the gear-box to slip as soon as any load was presented to it.

I preferred ANs to SNBs, but another occurrence put their love of me in doubt. Crawling in the Saturday afternoon traffic in Cheam Road, Sutton on a trip to Croydon, I was aware that the bus was continuing quite happily although I didn't have my foot on the accelerator. Operating the pedal by hand revealed that it was very stiff to release (they were generally stiff to apply so you would notice no difference). I lived with this problem through Sutton but by Carshalton it had got worse and quite dangerous.

At Wallington Green the 408/470 joined the 403 for a combined service to Croydon so I decided to remove the bus from service at that point with my passengers only having to wait about two minutes for a 403 to continue their journey. After seeing them all on their way I phoned the garage who asked me if I would mind bringing the bus home to save them coming out. This I agreed to, and returned via Belmont, A217, then across Epsom Downs and down into Epsom Town, as the traffic was lighter and kept moving, and it made a change.

'Showbus' AN 200 on a Sunday duty at Commercial Road, Guildford. *Author*

I was later informed that the problem was caused because the cab had just been painted and paint had run down between the pedal and the pivot and during its slow drying time had gradually got thicker and caused it all to seize up.

I also refused the SNB they gave me to finish the duty; it had been parked on full lock and there staring me in the face was this huge screw in the tyre. "Get some tea" they said "we'll sort you something out".

A BN on the 408 to Guildford and back – that must be a first, but where's my camera today?

Now the turn of a BN to misbehave. The retiring driver said "She drinks water, see how she goes, I've just filled her up." Nearing Boxhill steam was rising, no problem I thought I'll fill it at the garage up there. But would you believe that the garage was closed for lunch. A few houses past the garage I spotted a gentleman watering his roses with a hose. "Please could I pinch some of your water?" I asked. In fact he filled it for me, being happy to have some contact with a bus; perhaps a secret "anorak" there.

An easy mistake to make on single door ANs concerned the handbrake, or rather its unintentional use. The location of the handbrake control on the later ANs was not very well thought out, well not for me when not paying particular attention. It was very close to the control that operated the single front door. Just before stopping, to save time, one often operated the door control and once, and only once, I moved the adjacent control instead, which as I have already said is the handbrake; and air handbrakes are very sharp. I am pleased to report that I was not alone with this error.

One of my first trips after passing out, (look at the hair). A Sunday allocation on the 470 with an SNB (395) in place of an AN.

My son Barrie was now fourteen and at an age when he could come for a ride on Sundays and give his mother some peace. He was also very mechanically minded. If we had an AN, sometimes I would let him move the gear lever to the next position when told, and at the West Croydon turn he would sit in the cab and "fire her up" when ready.

Panic set in one time from the duty inspector; who when seeing this young boy starting the bus on his own, revving-up the engine to get the air up, assumed he was about to drive it away. He ran in front of the bus shouting "Stop, leave it there" etc. I did get a bit of a warning about that. But it was quite normal for drivers to take their offspring with them on a Sunday.

One Sunday Barrie remarked on how clean the bus was. Actually he was right but I hadn't really noticed. When I took it from the garage the fitter was still on it and made the remark, "Be careful, we need it tomorrow."

It later transpired that it had been designated the garage showbus, something that I had not heard of, and was to be at an event the next day, a Bank Holiday Monday.

YOU SHOULD ALWAYS CHECK

Without checking, one should never take a situation for granted and unfortunately that's what I, and to a greater degree, an old timer did one afternoon. And when I realised our mistake, it was almost too late.

In Leatherhead mid-afternoon, and only separated by one minute, there were two 470s that both came from Dorking. The first only went as far as Epsom, the second did the complete journey to West Croydon. Both buses had a changeover outside Taylor's shop in the High Street, so there I was waiting with Ben this old timer, happily talking to an old lady at the stop. Unusually the Croydon bus arrived first, and seeing this Ben said "Well here's mine," and quickly jumped in and was off. The road at this point could not support two parked buses without causing some blockage, so it was imperative to change quickly. The supposed "short" to Epsom was almost directly behind, but just out of sight around the corner. But when it came fully into view, I could then see it was also showing Croydon in the ultimate. A quick glance at the running plates told me it was not my bus but Ben's, who, without checking the plates had assumed that because the first one was showing Croydon that it was his bus. The previous driver had set it wrongly, I suppose assuming that all 470s went through to Croydon. The running card would have said 'ET', the code for Epsom Station or 'EC', for Epsom Clock Tower.

I hurriedly got in the seat and without setting up my ticket machine set off at a great rate of knots – which is not too dramatic in a single door AN. Luckily, Ben being first and advertising the destination of Croydon, picked up everyone around and I had a clear road, such that at Ashtead I managed to pin him in at a stop. The chore that followed was to change buses, the blinds, and of course any passengers who were going past Epsom.

The OAP tickets could be confusing, particularly the ones issued by Surrey County Council. Their area of validity was only within the jurisdiction of the SCC, and that was a bit different from the County boundaries. For example, Sutton was in Surrey, but under the jurisdiction of the Greater London Council, so theoretically you couldn't start the outward journey from there towards Croydon (also in the GLC area). You could go towards Epsom, provided you travelled past Cheam, because you were going into the SCC area. When I was actually issuing the ticket for a journey I always played it by the book, but when accepting a return issued by someone else, if it looked wrong, I always tried to explain the error but never refused the ticket, or charged any excess.

A VERY PERSONAL BUS SERVICE

"Take a National, go up to the town and then via the 408 road as far as Epsom," were my orders on a Saturday afternoon; "I've got another job for you after that." "There's been nothing through from Guildford or Dorking for over half an hour so expect some abuse." "What shall I do for the return?", I asked.

"I dunno, see what's going in the town," was his reply (referring to Epsom). On turning via Hook Road and Waterloo Road I approached the Clock Tower stop to be welcomed by a huge hoarde of waiting passengers. "There's been nothing here for ages," was the song as they viewed my blank destination display. "Where do you want to go?" I asked. "Ashtead; no Leatherhead – I want Grange Road" came the barrage of replies. "What about me?" said one solitary frail voice at the head of the queue, "I want the Wells Estate". "All right" I said, "This bus will go to Leatherhead, via Ashtead Village and then via the top road, basically a 479 but instead of via Lower Ashtead we'll go via the top road, so that we serve Grange Road for that lady." They couldn't believe it as I wound up non-existent (in Epsom anyway) 477 Leatherhead – a bus that runs for the passengers. At Leatherhead the Inspector was concerned that I was later than he hoped, but pleased about my initiative saying, "I s'pose they'll want that every Saturday now."

Most Sundays were quiet. The first 406 went out at 7.28, and when I was on instructions that day I generally got to the garage about then, just in case the rostered driver didn't turn up. Come 8.40, bossman was getting a bit twitchy about the second 406, supposed to depart at 8.21.

"Where is he?" I was asked as I sipped my tea standing in the conductors' room, "He phoned to say he'd be late but not this late." These two were in fact positioning journeys to Epsom for the 406 and ran in service. There were very few out of service journeys between Epsom and Leatherhead.

The banging on the window of the enquiry hatch revealed about a dozen potential passengers saying that they needed to get to Epsom soon or they would miss their special church service. "Where is the 8.20 406?" He looked at me; I guessed what he was thinking; I nodded.

"We will get you there," he told them as he turned to me, "get out something and run them down, Rod" he said. I hope they said a prayer thanking those two nice gentlemen at the bus company, one being the driver who even dropped them off outside their church in Church Street, which was not even on a bus route.

I NEVER GOT BORED

The staff canteen was open on Sundays but only from about 10.00 to 16.00 and if I had nothing else to do, sometimes I would help the volunteer staff.

The engineer in charge for the day appeared asking for special permission to bring non-staff into the canteen. A long distance coach had a mechanical problem and the driver had brought it in for attention. We had plenty of provisions so it was all cooks to the tea urn. At my suggestion we did however charge them a bit more than the usual very subsidised low prices; it boosted the social club funds a bit. Even with that they got a very good deal, and left quite happy after about an hour.

Approaching the Burford Bridge stop from Mickleham with a 470 bound for Dorking, the retardation of the AN was not quite what I had in mind, although my foot was flat on the floor. According to the gauges all the pressures are OK. Oh well continue, but be wary. All the way to Croydon and back to Leatherhead it never failed again. Must be me again I thought, but I told the driver who took it off me in The Crescent, Leatherhead. A lot of them like that, he told me, you just have to know how to drive them.

Next day in the canteen he wasn't so chirpy. At that very same stop it did exactly the same, only he wasn't so lucky, he hit a delivery van gently in the rear.

A far from smooth ride though wasn't one I gave one evening on leaving Guildford. This wonderful AN had no 1st gear and it had very poor guts. Pulling away and turning left at the lights into the High Street was a location where 1st would be needed. This evening with no 1st, and no guts we just sat there, the engine making a chugging noise barely above tickover. Twice the lights changed to our advantage. I then shouted, "Hold on tight," as I revved it in neutral then slammed it into 2nd at the same time letting off the handbrake. We crawled very, very slowly but we made it.

One of the late night 408s had a very long layover in Guildford and the card said to take the bus to Guildford garage where one could sample their wonderful refreshments (from a machine). I had unsuccessfully tried to find Guildford garage once before in the dark, missing the very narrow road and ended up trying to find a suitable turning point. So this night I stayed in Commercial Road, drank my own coffee, listened quietly to my radio, then promptly fell asleep. It was about ten minutes after the official departure time that I was awakened by the banging on the door by some irate passengers who had spotted me in the first seat of the SNB; sorry folks.

Sometimes the job could bring some humour and this would have gone down well on the TV series, with probably the best 'serves you right to a passenger'. It occurred during my last week. Things were quiet on the disruption front and I was asked to ride 'shot-gun' for a new driver who was unsure of the 408 route to West Croydon. He was a lovely fellow, very polite, but his driving was very erratic and jerky in our single door AN, and probably not helped by my presence either.

So, picture this. The location was West Croydon bus station; the time, late one Saturday afternoon where passengers were returning with loads of shopping. One overdressed lady boarded the bus, dragging her well loaded shopping trolley behind her. She paid her fare and dumped herself a short way down the lower deck of the single door AN, and in doing so partially blocked the gangway with the trolley, making it difficult for other passengers to pass. Our new driver spotted this, left his cab and very politely asked her if she would mind moving it. The reply suggested she would leave it where she pleased and that he should concentrate on driving the bus. I beckoned him to leave it alone and return to the cab, as I didn't want him becoming distressed at the confrontation.

A few minutes later, and an oldish man boarded accompanied by a large black labrador dog, and asked if it was OK to bring him on board, and could they please stay downstairs. No problem said our driver. The man thanked him and proceeded down the bus squeezing past the trolley.

Other interesting loans were these Daimler Fleetlines from Bournemouth Corporation. Initially passengers were confused by their bright yellow livery and unusual blind displays but they had time to get used to them because they stayed 2½ years. The location is West Croydon . *J.G.S. Smith*

Now dogs of course have a good sense of smell and there was something very tasty in that trolley and he decided 'to bag' it. By the way, male dogs 'bag' things by cocking their leg, and madam wasn't very pleased at the dampening of her trolley. Anyway, off we went across the lights and down towards Reeves Corner, where along the way some person in a car pulled out of a side turning . Our new driver overreacted with the brakes, the bus nose-dived and the aforementioned shopping trolley took off on its own towards the front of the bus and deposited its contents in the front door footwell; luckily the door was closed. The chain of events was more than the driver could stand. He had to wipe the tears from his eyes before continuing. By now the bus was in total hilarity. Because of her arrogant way to the polite driver, there was no sympathy. As the passengers started to laugh one was heard to say "Serves her right for being so bloody rude." She sat po faced to Trembath Corner where she departed. "Goodnight Madam" – "Cheeky sod" was the reply.

At Clandon another potentially awkward lady boarded complaining that she had been waiting over 45 minutes for a bus, and where had we been? I carefully explained that on that section of the route buses ran at sixty minute intervals and she had obviously missed the previous one by 15 minutes. This she accepted and actually apologised, luckily not realising that I myself was actually a good ten minutes late.

We didn't often wind up passengers, but one case comes to mind and really I just fell in with what another driver had started. I was due to take over a bus outside the garage, which turned out to be an elderly SNC. On boarding, the driver looked at me and said in a loud voice so that all the passengers could hear. "Oh! it's you, the new boy, do you know how to drive this bus? "No, not really, but I'll have a good try," I said in an equally loud voice as I sat down in the driver's seat, which being on one of the early ones could swivel round to face the incoming passengers, and had been left in that posi-tion. "This will be awkward," I said, "all the way to Kingston like this, I'll soon get a stiff neck, who on earth designed this bus?" "Don't worry about that you're not going to Kingston anyway," "No, where to then?" "Croydon, do you know the way?" "Don't be silly, Croydon has big buses, this is a little one," I said as I opened the destination box to look at the display. "You're right" I said, "can you draw me a map?" "No problem old chap, always will-ing to help" as he picked up a used Almex ticket from the floor (which were about 2 inches square), and began scribbling on it and giving instructions for the scribble. "You OK now?" he said on the steps. "No, how do you start it up? Oh! Never mind, I've found it". The old chap in the first front seat then came meekly forward and offered his assistance in getting to Epsom, where he said he gets off. I explained that the other driver was only trying to wind us all up, and enjoyed my type of response, which was probably better than what he was expecting. At least his wife saw the funny side – probably explained to him later.

TIME TO MOVE ON

My personal business of radio repairing had picked up tremendously, so much so that it was getting difficult to cope with the demand in the spare time available. It was a great shame to leave the buses, as I enjoyed my two completely different life styles.

I had met a lot of new friends both working colleagues and passengers, who contrary to common belief weren't all bad, and as you've probably gathered from what I have written, if you treat people in a certain way, usually (but not always) the response is favourable. My old Gran who had a lot of influence in bringing me up, used to say, "Treat people the way you would expect to be treated yourself and at times put yourself in their place, and you won't go too wrong." My resignation was not unexpected by the GTS who wished me well. The last duty of the day was on the 416/462 with a BN.

IN REMEMBRANCE

After leaving the buses, when time allowed, I would visit my old conductor mate Harry (photograph on page 32). That man who some years previously had taken me, the novice driver, under his wing and shown me the ropes.

My partner in my radio repair business had himself become ill and our partnership finished, so I had taken a job as a technical sales representative, where at Christmas it was normal to distribute scotch to my customers.

I considered Harry would be more grateful than some greedy purchasing manager, so one was re-directed his way. I can't remember the name of that company in Kingston Road, Leatherhead that I wrote on the "gifts delivered to" list, but the sales manager was one H. Ranger!

Then one day I had a phone call from his youngest daughter telling me of his illness, "The Big C", and his awaiting admittance to hospital.

My first visit to him at the Marsden Hospital, Belmont, initially gave me a terrific shock. I had been given the location of his bed, and on entering the dimly lit room I could see that the occupant was very thin in the face and extremely white. Harry was well built, some said like an ox. My god, I thought, he's gone downhill very quickly, poor chap he's near the end. At that moment I heard him call from across the room; he was sitting up in a chair, having been moved to a different bed. Harry was not the kind of person to let anything get the better of him easily.

You may remember I remarked that during my spell as his mate, on many occasions he would bring in vegetables for me and his work mates, these being grown in one of his five allotments. When he was in hospital, some of his gardening mates got together and partially looked after some of them. On his release one of his first chores was to go to back to his allotments.

Unfortunately, even his stamina and will-power couldn't win over that terrible disease, and one of my best friends ever passed away some time later.

A bus was used to take some of the many mourners to the crematorium – possibly the bus service suffered for a while that day, but for good reason.

THE CHISWICK EXPERIENCE

I have had many jobs in my life, and in early 1983 it was the turn of Pioneer hi-fi to suffer my presence. My job title was "Technical Support Engineer", and my main duties were answering queries relating to the company's sound and video equipment, both by telephone and letter and calming irate customers who often told me they thought the Pioneer product was rubbish, which was not true.

One day a repair technician showed me an advert in a newspaper for a job vacancy at Chiswick Bus Works as a unit manager, and did I think he had a chance of getting it? Actually I thought no, but me, maybe. So I applied and was granted an interview at Chiswick. Some friends who worked for LT advised me not to mention any earlier connection with buses, or bus preservation, as some people in LT had a dislike of "bus anoraks," so I did as advised.

As was usual with London Transport, the interview was conducted by what was known as a 'panel'. These were about six persons who had a different subject interest in the applicant. I was very surprised at how little technical interest there was, as the interview centred round my management experience. After the interview I was ushered out of the office, but left to my own devices to find my way out of the site. Now that *was* a rather daft thing to do.

From an early age it was always my aim to get into that famous bus works, and during school holidays with friends I would sometimes go there, but the nearest we could get was standing at the gates with a pair of binoculars, or waiting patiently across the road for some movement. This now was my great chance for a look around; just supposing I don't get the job, it would have been a missed opportunity; I had to take it. So I took the best and longest route, which included a view of the skid patch and the back road where many buses were parked, then doubled back to the main gate. I walked with a very authoritative style passing many people, none of whom questioned my presence.

You can't imagine my feelings (or perhaps you can) when a few days later I received a phone call to say I had been successful. So on 18th July 1983 after a short visit to head office at 55 Broadway to collect my travel pass, I made my way to Gunnersbury on a D78 District Line train, and with just a nod to the security man, proudly walked into the Chiswick site.

My position at Chiswick was as one of four Section Engineers, and it was our job to ensure that all the repairable items requested by both Aldenham and the garages were fulfilled; my responsibility was initially just for bus radios which were delivered by the small teams who toured the various garages and removed faulty radios from buses. They replaced them with repaired ones from the float they kept on their vans. Not all the radios were interchangeable; generally they only had radio channels fitted applicable to their garage or district (i.e., Cardinal, Tower, etc.).

Soon after my joining, we started repairing what is known as a "gearbox translator panel". This is a box of electronics that controls the operation of an automatic gearbox. It looks at various parameters, like vehicle road speed and throttle or brake demand, then instructs the gearbox accordingly. The first types we tackled were for Titan and LS 3 vehicles (Red Arrows) but soon followed the standard LS, and then the famous Voith, as mainly fitted to Metrobuses.

For Titans and Voith we had a piece of test gear called a "Beaver". This test equipment had been designed and built by the electronic development section and was really just a big piece of electronics that compared what the panel under test gave with parameters loaded to the Beaver by a cassette tape. Most comparisons related to gear change points and throttle dip periods, both of which were adjustable, either by a variable potentiometer or by changing fixed resistors.

Voith was a German company, whose design of the panel was a lot more complicated. The company wanted to do the repairs to their panels "in house", believing that only they could do it to the required high standard. However part of the purchase agreement was that we would repair our own panels and that Voith would supply all the necessary data to allow that to happen, which they did. However I had to sign a declaration from Voith that I would not pass anything over to any other party.

If a section engineer was absent for any reason, one of us others would stand in; so I soon found myself overseeing on a management level items such as engine repair, radiators and gearboxes. It wasn't very difficult acting in that capacity, as all the sections had foreman and charge-hands who were more than capable of running the show.

Life at Chiswick was so different from anything else I had met in outside industry. On returning home on the first day, my wife enquired how many worked there. In typical "Lucas" fashion, the reply of, Oh! About half of them, was, on reflection a bit over estimated. However the repairs that left Chiswick were to a meticulously high standard; there just didn't seem to be any rush to increase the output quantity.

Most of my first day was taken up with being given a good official tour of the works and meeting some colleagues, but as some of the works was on summer shutdown, it was rather quiet.

My tour guide was Ron Pinnock, foreman of what was known as "Bus Lighting" but where all the little items like switches, wiper and heater motors were also repaired. During our tour he enquired where I lived. When I replied "Tadworth," he said, "Oh, you can use the Reigate Staff Bus", (which actually went further on to Woodhatch, to drop off and collect two staff members). "It goes near Tadworth." But on enquiring for permission from Personnel to ride on it, I was told I was not eligible as it was only for factory personnel, and me being manager grade didn't qualify. They did hint that the final decision rested with the actual drivers. So off to find the drivers; one Mick an Inspector, worked in 'Strip and Clean', the section that dismantled, cleaned and generally prepared units ready for inspection and repair; the other, Tony worked in the Experimental shop. "No problem," exclaimed Mick, saying the more the merrier, it makes it look needed.

There were three staff buses, and as it was customary for the Reigate one to be first out, it was at the head of the queue. The others went to Sidcup and Catford.

Our bus was RMA 36, a former British European Airways Routemaster with a front entrance. These originally had the big 11.3 litre engine fitted, but ours like many had been exchanged for a standard 9.6 (AEC of course). This change didn't seem to affect its performance much, but I think the fuel pump had been opened up a bit. However because it still had the high speed differential fitted it could manage about 65mph, but most starts required the use of 1st gear.

Off we went at 16.10 hrs, turning left into Chiswick High Road, then first right, which after a few wiggles, led us to the A4 in the London direction. Approaching Hammersmith we turned right and went over Hammersmith Bridge, then up to Roehampton where we joined the A3. We managed a good

A view from my office window, shows an Atlantean in ex London Country South East colours, with many of the body panels replaced. At the top right is the famous Chiswick clock, situated on the tower that formed part of the main canteen roof.

turn of speed on the downhill slope past the old KLG factory and along the A3, only losing a bit on the Malden flyover. Then left towards Worcester Park where we dropped off a few, like-wise in Cheam Village, where once through, we turned right onto the A217 towards Reigate. I jumped off at Tadworth roundabout. I say "jumped" because it seemed customary not actually to stop but slow down just enough for persons to make a leap for it.

The next morning I waited for the bus at 6.15 at the same location. We took a slightly different route on the inward journey around Gunnersbury, because the entry to the works was only possible in one direction from Chiswick High Road.

Some years later one of the drivers asked if I could repair his music centre, and it was agreed that on the way in one morning he would drop it off at my house which is on the B2032, the road that runs parallel to the A217. From that day on the bus always went that way, so I had a door-to-door service on the way in.

We arrived at Chiswick at around 7.10 ready for breakfast in the main canteen, but because of my management status, this was the only meal I was allowed to take in that canteen; for the mid-day one I had to use the "Executive" one behind the main one. I didn't ever take an early breakfast, but instead usually joined my colleagues in a small office in the centre of the works, where tea was made by a nice lady who also looked after the vast number of cats that lived on the site.

The buildings that formed the radio/electronics shop were two newish 'Portakabins' joined together. I had an office at one end, which conveniently looked out directly onto the road coming up from 'the Dip', meaning that all day, I could see what was going around the site on test.

The only problem with these Portakabins was their lack of insulation, as in the summer they got unbearably hot, and in the winter could be freezing cold in the morning. We got over this though, by leaving the electric heaters on all night, using the excuse that it keeps the electronic test gear at a sensible temperature, and therefore ready for use first thing in the morning. This was only half right, but since no-one else seemed to know anything about electronics, my statement was never challenged.

Another problem was the actual siting of the cabins. They were near to a huge drain with a cover that did not fit very well and often the smell of effluent meant that whilst it was being attended to, we had to evacuate the building and retire to the canteen.

In my office, the winter cold problem was often helped by putting a small quantity of scotch in my coffee which we made from our own kettle. This beverage I shared with my clerk. One morning early, the works manager came in to see me and commented that he could smell something odd (the coffee and scotch mix). I said it must be my new cough mixture, to which he replied that he must come and try some, as it smells more appetising than his!

The famous "Dip" was closed on this occasion because of the high water level. To the rear can be seen the "Experimental Shop", and to the left, the main factory. *Author*

Ex West Midlands Titan, now numbered T 1128 was being used in October 1984 for tuition on how to correctly do a recovery lift. This was brought about following the increasing number of buses being damaged during such a recovery, which was usually caused because the lift was too high, causing the rear to drag along the road under certain conditions. *Author*

My clerk (Dick) whose job it was to look after our little local stores was a great asset to me, and knew how to "work the system". During a morning cuppa, I asked him if he knew the local area, and whether there were any shops where I could buy a 2 inch paint brush. About an hour later one appeared on my desk. On questioning Dick, he said it came from another shop's stores; we didn't have paint brushes in our stores, but we did have radio batteries, which apparently were good bartering material for swapping for paint brushes.

My immediate responsibility was for a staff of seven, a bunch with mixed backgrounds and capabilities. Four had previously worked in the bus lighting shop and had been given radio repair jobs because they had a "knowledge" of radio, or so they said. In fact on my first day one of them asked me what I knew about radio, and following my reply he said, "Yes maybe, but you haven't worked on these, all radios are different you know" – silly man.

Two of the staff were two almost identical black twins, difficult to tell apart, and unfortunately – despite being excellent engineers – seemed a bit over-concerned about their colour. I was told that in the past, whenever there was any reprimanding, they often fell back on the "you're only picking on me 'cause I'm black", reasoning. This attitude annoys, mainly because I don't really care about anyone's colour, race or religion. Let's face it, there are lots of white people whom other white people don't care for much. Of the other staff, one was a "radio ham", and had an acute knowledge of all types of radio.

There was much staff unrest, but this went back a long way, with the belief that they were being sold off etc. This revolved around a theory that their services could be minimised, and therefore some of them displaced, with their place being taken by a piece of electronic equipment that would diagnose faults in the radios. In part it did have some substance, but only in the same way that diagnostic equipment was already being used to aid the repair of gear control panels. Engineers would still be needed to implement the required component replacement, and control the test equipment.

The distrust of managers before me was such that my office had been bugged with a small microphone hidden behind a cupboard, and a cable threaded underneath the cabins back to a work area, where it fed an amplifier and earphones. I found this very early on, but didn't let on, and instead often set up fake discussions with another colleague from the design section. Later on when they began to trust me they removed the device.

Chiswick, like many establishments had open days, and to celebrate the Golden Jubilee, both Chiswick and the near-by Acton railway works held a joint venture over the weekend of the 2nd and 3rd July 1983 to celebrate the fiftieth anniversary of the coming into being of London Transport. This event was about a fortnight before I actually worked there, so I attended just as a visitor and drove Cobham Bus Museum's T 448 to it.

On 11th August 1985 another open day was staged and promoted as the Chiswick Bus Festival. This like the previous event was hugely popular, with large crowds attending, and to this one I drove Cobham bus museum's RML 3. I remember how proud I was when the public address commentator remarked on how well I had parked it first go and very neatly in the space that had been left for it between RM 2 and RMC 4. I was not officially involved with the event, so had a good chance to enjoy it.

Probably the biggest item of interest was as usual the famous skid patch, but not far behind was 'Drive-a-bus', where visitors were allowed to drive buses along the back road of the works. For this, several RM-type vehicles were provided, with the instructor hanging out of the cab next to the driver. I believe there were a few knocks where drivers argued with the old railway sleepers that marked out the road, but nothing too bad.

RMC 1473 on skid demonstration duties on the 11th August 1985 open day. Note the red flag, which flew when the 'patch' was in use for the skid. According to the garage plate the bus was allocated to Chalk Farm garage. *Author*

The cab, numbered RT 1962, of the Simulbus.

Another item that received a great interest was the 'Simulbus', a simulator used for driving tuition. The actual driver interface was housed in a mock up cab, and labelled RT 1962. Within the cab, were a driver's seat, a steering wheel, a conventional RT style pre-selector gear lever, and three pedals. All these items were connected via some very basic electrics to a control system. The cab faced a large screen, behind which was a rotating table containing a model of a street scene, which included many roads, crossings, buildings, zebra crossings, other vehicles, along with all the street furniture to be found on a normal road. The 'bus' was a movable stylus, on an arm, steered by the signals received from the actual steering wheel. The total visual effect was what you would see from the driver's seat.

The speed was effectively the rotational speed of the turntable and was derived from the brake and accelerator pedals. The sound of an engine corresponding to this speed was relayed through a loudspeaker. Visitors were allowed to 'drive' the bus for a timed period.

Fixing a poster on a bus was a popular attraction for the younger generation, probably because it meant sloshing water about, so they tended to get wet. For all the special events, small charges were made, with the money being donated to a charity.

London Transport had a mass of clubs for its employees, and many were centred on the Chiswick site. The one I loved was the model railway club, which I only became aware of on the open day, when it opened its doors to the public. It was situated in the huge basement under the main training building, and was mainly OO-gauge, but an N-gauge area was under construction. Much of the layout could not be seen from any location as it was masked by the supports for the building above.

There was a beautiful street scene that boasted an electric tramway, with a church at one end where a newly married couple stood on the steps. Religious music emanated from a small loudspeaker in the tower. The track was standard Peco style, but the scenery was fantastic.

Rolling stock was a mixture of ready-to-run and kit-built, but there were also some models built from scratch with plastic card. Chiswick had a fair share of very talented model makers.

Another equally leisurely interest was outdoor bowls, and for this a beautiful green was maintained along with a club house complete with veranda. I noticed that in later years when the Chiswick site was being dismantled, the turf was being dug up by certain individuals, probably for their own lawn. The important thing was that it went to a good home.

The Voith company were very keen to improve the quality of both their gearboxes and the electronic panels that controlled them, and to further this regular meetings took place either at Chiswick or the Voith offices at Thornton Heath.

I accompanied Colin Curtis the vehicle engineering manager, to these in my capacity as works electronics engineer.

One item on the agenda at one such meeting was the scrapping of a complete Metrobus gearbox. The gearbox in question was received into the works in the normal way, but when the top cover was removed it revealed a substance rather like a thick solid blancmange. Voith gearboxes run extremely hot and as a result the lubrication oil is one that possesses a high temperature specification; someone had used Routemaster gearbox oil, which does not. As much as we tried, the gearbox could not be dismantled, the baked oil had effectively locked all the gears and clutches together.

Staff within my section were split into two groups, and were known as either 'radio craftsmen', or 'electronic craftsmen', both hourly paid and they only worked on either radios or electronic items, they were not allowed to mix their work, even though technically they were quite capable. The work input for each discipline was very unpredictable; there might be a high influx of radios and no electronics work, or vice-versa, but because of the rules they were not allowed to help each other out. This was a not very efficient way of working and I discussed it with them, saying that in outside industry they would be considered technical staff. It received a favourable reception, and jointly we agreed on a solution. So I started negotiations with the works manager for dual technician status, which also included staff status, enhanced travel and pension rights and a shorter working week. Eventually it was agreed and was implemented, but not before huge objections from their trade union.

So there I had a shop full of technical staff, repairing whatever came in. Good thing really, because the work was starting to increase. Metros, Titans and Nationals were now a few years old and lots of their little electronic units were starting to fail, so much that an extra member of staff was required, and he came in the shape of Wally from Bus Lighting. Wally had previously repaired all the gear control panels used on RM, SMS, MB and DMS variants. This work had to be done outside our shop in the bus lighting shop, because there was no room to house the enormous test gear.

In typical old LT fashion, to replicate what a bus produced and required, the test gear was built from genuine bus parts. It had a speed sensitive generator under the bench, and this was driven by a motor whose speed could be varied. On the front it had two huge meters, each about 18 inches in diameter; one displayed the rpm of the generator, the other the supposed road speed.

Wally was also a good intricate mechanical man and was soon put to work on the mechanics of Voith gear selector switches.

Next to where Wally used to sit was a very nice inspector who hailed from India. On returning a bit late from lunch one day, I spotted that he had his tool drawer open and a mains cable was falling from it. He became very embarrassed when I got close and tried to close the drawer, "What's that" I asked, as he gingerly opened it to reveal an electric clothes iron in pieces. "I was mending it for someone in my lunch break and it has over run, Sir." "Well," I said, "you'd better get on and finish it," and just walked away. His local foreman then came forward and asked what was he up to, and when told, asked if I wanted him disciplined? "Don't be silly man," I said, "one day I might want mine mended."

It somehow got suggested that I might get involved and test some of the modifications that were being done on bus transmission characteristics. The development section was investigating what was necessary to modify the change points, neutral gap and throttle delay timings of the few Titans at Catford (TL) garage, that had been delivered from new with either TL11 (a Leyland Turbo charged engine) or L11, in place of the normal Gardner engine. It was thought that the performance of both could be improved with a change to these settings.

Using some basic theory about the engines' different performances, two panels were modified prior to taking them to Catford, where road testing took place. A few minor changes were then made, but the overall conclusion from the vehicle engineering manager (Mr Curtis) was that the slight improvements obtained were not worth the bother. This decision was also influenced by all the complications of holding a small stock of different items.

The L11 engine wasn't up to much, but the TL11 engine, which was also fitted to many long distance coaches, actually revved a lot higher than the Gardner, and could deliver a lot more output if the fuel pump settings allowed. The London Country LR class proved that, but unfortunately that extra power and higher rev capacity was never really made use of, because it was fitted with a close ratio gearbox.

This Non-LT Bristol LH has had its front wheels replaced by a set of flanged wheels for use on a railway track. The steering on a normal road is done via two pairs of small wheels.

Left A close up of the arrangement. The rear wheels appear to remain as built for road use. *Author*

A long time later when Bus Engineering Ltd (BEL) was formed we actually modified an ex National Bus Olympian. The customer wanted to use it on excursions, and his drivers were complaining it would only do 43mph. A wide ratio gearbox accompanied by a higher ratio differential solved that, and gave a maximum speed of about 58mph; the drivers thought it wonderful, and guess what, the fuel consumption was drastically reduced. But what about the brakes, one may ask?

The seed was sown, my PSV driving licence from the past was still current so there should be no problem with me driving buses, but hey! not so fast. Everyone who needed to drive an LT vehicle was assessed by them, even for private cars, and although I still had a current PSV licence, I still had to go through the training school. Chiswick believed that no-one else trained to their high standards, and to a degree this was correct.

I asked the progress manager (who was also my boss at that time) if he could approve me getting tuition from the driving school, which he did. The speed at which it was done was probably helped by three factors.

One, in my workshops, I had repaired several personal hi-fis belonging to the instructors, second I used to dine with one of the training managers, and third, and the official one, was that the trainer RMs had been fitted with a facility to save the instructor shouting to the trainee. The system consisted of a microphone mounted close to where he sat, an amplifier which derived its operating voltage from the cab light socket and a small loudspeaker hanging in the cab. This unit had been designed and fitted by one of the instructors, and the training school wanted some professional assurance (from me) that this supposed amateur had done things safely; in general he had.

The most important things to watch are first adequate fusing, close to the source of the supply, and second to remember that RMs have a 'floating' supply. This means that unlike most cars, neither polarity of the battery supply is connected to the body frame. However, it is usual in the design of amplifiers, that one side of the supply is connected to the earth, and this is usually negative. Therefore, one can see that if a metal bodied microphone is used (and for screening purposes, its body is earthed to the amplifier earth) and it touches a metal part of the bus, then the bus will be connected to that earth polarity, whatever it is.

It is not unknown for 'floating earth' buses like the Routemaster to have an earth, caused by a short between one polarity and the bus body – lampholders are a frequent cause of that – but often it doesn't matter, until that is that the other polarity is also earthed.

So to sum up, if the bus already has a positive earth, and a metal microphone which is earthed to negative is being used, if you touch the microphone to the bus body, you would get a bang, or even weld the microphone to the bus. The answer: use plastic bodied microphones and no metal bodied in-line plugs either. This shows the importance of correct fusing.

Some special paint jobs. RMs 781 and 359 prepared for advertising 'Pepsi'. *Author*

But back to the driving. The first move was, "See what he's like and then decide what to do". And guess what? and I couldn't believe it, they put me up in a Green RMC. After all those years, I'm back at home again.

After a few bits of instruction out of the gate we went, then followed the route the staff buses took to the A4 and returned by Turnham Green. "Have you driven one before?," I was asked on the return trip. Actually I pretended to be concentrating on the road and not hear him.

Along with this driving tuition I had an ulterior motive, if only I could pull it off. I was by now very involved with the London Bus Preservation people at Cobham Bus Museum, who had within their collection several buses which my PSV licence didn't cover. My licence stated "Any type PSV automatic transmission only", i.e., double or single deck, it also had a manual gearbox section but that limited me to single deck vehicles and a maximum length of 27ft 6ins; remember I took it in a BN with London Country, who to stop the drivers that they had trained going off to drive touring coaches (that were a lot longer), generally only tested you on a vehicle necessary for the actual garage requirements. There were though a few who were lucky, and were tested on double decks known as 'Yellow Perils'. I would dearly like to be able to drive anything with a manual gearbox. For that, the licence classification was "Any type PSV".

No matter what anyone tells you, in life, it's who you know, and as I've already said, I mingled with some very useful people. In casual conversation about my proposed training, I said, "Could I not somehow get re-tested (yet again) but on a double deck vehicle with manual transmission?" The big problem I was told was that London Transport didn't own or have access to any such vehicles. "What," I said, "if I could get such a vehicle?" "OK you get a vehicle and we'll lend you an instructor for two afternoons only, just to brush you up a bit."

There was a shortage of instructors who knew about driving a bus with manual transmission and the slight variations in the actual test requirements. Cobham agreed I could use their open topper, a Leyland PD2 ex Southport and now roofless.

On the allocated day, I took the instructor to Cobham in my 1963 Mini, and after checking the bus over, I drove it to Weybridge Station where we stopped. His initial comments concerned my snatchy gear changes, so I asked if he would like to have a drive, to get an understanding of the vehicle's characteristics. After a few miles of wrestling with this gearbox, that initially tended to be a bit stiff, he refrained from any more comments on that subject, and instead concentrated on a few of my bad habits that I had picked up over the years.

The actual test was in the environs of Walton-on-Thames, where in the centre, I encountered three hazards.

It seems that whenever I take a PSV test, something out of the ordinary happens. Today, I misunderstood the examiner's poor directions in the town regarding where he wanted me to go, and so got in the wrong traffic lane in the one-way system. I was, though, very pleased with the way I corrected it and got across two lanes of moving traffic.

The next episode happened sitting at the traffic lights. Because it was a very hot day, I had the cab sliding window open, and this lovely old gentleman leant on the front mudguard and proceeded to tell me that he remembered the bus when it was in Southport, and asked where was it now.

It was just like the final scene in the film *Genevieve*, where that old chap talks to the character played by John Gregson about the car when it had been stopped by a policeman at a road junction. It nearly caused Genevieve to lose the bet between him and the character played by Kenneth Moore, on who could get to London first. My examiner seeing this happening, shouted, "Get rid of him;" not so easy with him in contact with the bus.

We traversed the town and returned to the same spot, luckily the old gent had gone, but in his place the traffic lights had failed, and it was a free for all. Once again I was quite pleased with my dealing with the situation. But not so though with me trying to get reverse, for the reversing around a corner bit. To get reverse on that bus, you forced the lever towards second and lifted it over the interlock, which allowed it to go close to the cab side wall. On these Leylands, there is a cable loom that runs along the cab wall under the sliding window, and it is held in place by a metal cable clip which can be very sharp. In selecting reverse, it is all too easy to catch your knuckles on, and yes, I did – blood everywhere. I made sure he didn't see it though – he might have condemned the bus for being unsafe!

Anyway, I passed.

The next day, back at Chiswick to continue with the type training, we found a Metrobus; I had never before driven a Metro, but because I had repaired its transmission electronic panels, was fully aware of the transmission characteristics.

The gearbox is fitted with an integral retarder, which provided a method of braking almost divorced from the foundation brakes – the normal ones. Under initial braking the retarder does most of the work. However, this retarder only works in the higher gears and not 1st. This is because the retarder uses the torque converter for its operation. The torque converter is also used when the gearbox is in 1st, and it can't do two jobs at once, so the retarder loses out – it has to otherwise there would be no 1st gear.

This is what happens. Imagine the bus is moving at 35mph, is coasting and you are using the footbrake to slow down. As it does so, the gearbox will (on a three-speed Voith) change from 3rd gear to 2nd as the road speed decreases, then as the road speed reduces even more, the gearbox will change to 1st gear. You can see that as you are braking, you have a working retarder assisting the foundation brakes in 3rd and 2nd, but as soon as the box goes into 1st, the retarder drops out and you are suddenly only on foundation brakes which weren't doing much before, so the braking effect appears reduced. This effect can be a bit disconcerting at first, but all you have to do is apply more pressure on the footbrake.

Off we went on a similar route as with the RMC. I found the Metro a bit of a sloppy bus, it seemed to wander a bit, but the driving method and road positioning to use were similar to the ANs that I had driven for many miles some years previously.

Next up was the Bristol LH single decker, the BL. BLs have some similarities with London Country's BNs, which I had previously driven; but are a bit longer, are 8ft wide, but most importantly are fitted with power steering and a semi-automatic gearbox. I must be a bit weird, but I quite liked them; nobody else seemed to. We started from outside the training school and headed towards the gate, just before though, my question of how far are we going, was met with, "If you can manage a Metro, I'm damn sure you can manage this."

It was also noted that I should be type trained on an RT vehicle, because one was attached to the radio section. This bus, RT 2958, had been converted to a mobile workshop, and had many aerials fitted to allow their performances to be compared, and to measure field strength of the radio signals around the network.

For this I had a different instructor, and we borrowed the skid bus (if the memory is right it was RT 1530) which wasn't licensed for road use, so the training consisted of a few trips around the works.

My instructor admitted that it had been many years since he had actually driven a pre-selector, and gave a brief instruction of what to do, and then proceeded to give a most terrible demonstration. Getting out he said, "Well, you see if you can do better." After my almost perfect drive, he asked had I driven one before, and following my reply said I should have told him so. This I had decided not to do, just in case I had made a terrible mess; we became good friends.

To do my survey of the RM amplifying equipment, it was suggested that to save disrupting the RM training buses at Chiswick, I go to North Weald aerodrome, where some spare vehicles were parked.

"Training" had an office there, and used some of the closed runways for novice drivers to get the feel of a bus. The first trip to North Weald, near Epping in Essex, would incorporate my Titan type training.

For my "type training" I was assigned Bill Wingen, an ex-German prisoner of war who heralded originally from Dresden, which after the war was put into the Eastern Bloc. He had no family left there, and had made several friends here, so he remained in England and made a new life.

His first job was driving trolleybuses at Isleworth. Bill was a typical old-fashioned polite German gentleman; he always knocked on my office door before entering, shook my hand and almost clicked his heels and bowed.

Bill confided in me that he had been forced into the Hitler youth movement, then during the war was put in the Luftwaffe flying Messerschmitts, but not being a very ruthless person it worried him, so somehow got transferred to training the pilots.

Yours truly with Bill Wingen

That also didn't agree much with his health, so he was given a job as a motor-cycle dispatch rider and transferred to the front in France, where one afternoon late on in the war, he realised he was surrounded and decided to surrender – but not before trading his motorcycle for a good evening meal with a French farmer! Unfortunately he surrendered to the Canadians, who gave him a bit of a rough time. But, as he said "That's war."

My type training on the RML was also done by going to North Weald, but it was a fair way from Chiswick. Going together as we often did, Bill would be ribbed about his bombing raids during the war and was asked if he ever bombed that site, but it was all taken in good humour.

My only mistake I remember in type training related to the RML. I was driving it in 'manual over-ride' and had stopped with the gear lever in 3rd gear position. On releasing the handbrake when pulling away the bus rolled backwards. Something for me to note was that when stationary and the gear lever is in 3rd the system gives neutral.

Once doing the training on a National, I nearly got done for speeding. We were going via the A40, which is quite a nice open road, but has a 40mph speed limit. The National was quite happy purring along, keeping up with other traffic, all doing about 47mph; the Instructor was seemingly content with my driving.

On stopping at the traffic lights at Hillingdon, two motor-cycle cops stopped alongside me, where one waved to attract my attention, and then proceeded to tap his speedo, as a warning to watch my speed. The bus had nothing on it to advertise that it was a training vehicle, merely 'Private' on the front blind. Close one, that!

I became a bit of a victim of the system, as according to Bill Love the senior skid instructor, the rules stated that skid training must be done before type training, and I had missed out on the skid. With a lot of coaxing he eventually calmed down, allocated a skid instructor to me, and said I would be done in a few days' time.

The consumption of alcohol was allowed whilst on duty, and in fact Chiswick works main canteen had a licensed bar at one end, where subsidised beverages could be purchased in the lunch break.

I preferred to do my drinking away from the works and on most Fridays it was commonplace for the progress manager and me to go to the pub on Turnham Green for a 'couple of jars' and put the world right.

The next Friday when retuning from such an occasion, and walking past the training school, a shout came from the doorway, "Rod, fancy doing your skid now?" I explained about the two pints but that fell on deaf ears, with the comment "You'll be OK." Who was I to argue? After all, weren't they the experts? So after a quick visit to the gents it was round the back to find the RM skid bus.

Skid training is really teaching the art of skid prevention, and if you got that wrong, skid control. I was told that by using cadence braking, one shouldn't really get into the skid situation in the first place. The instructor showed the principle of cadence braking, which is simply pushing the pedal down to get heavy braking, then just before the wheels are about to lock up, releasing it quickly; the process being repeated many times. The principle is similar to a manual version of ABS.

The purpose of all this is to keep the front wheels turning, because they will not steer the bus if they are not revolving. The required end result was to stop the bus safely in one of the yellow boxes painted on the road, the way up to which is very slippery because the surface is smooth and it is continuously being flooded with water.

The dramatic bit shown on the films of a bus spinning is what happens when you get it wrong; the instructor deliberately does it to frighten the hell out of you. Frightened initially you may be, but you soon realise that there is very little sensation that the bus is actually spinning, and this is because you are at the pivotal point – the bus is spinning around you.

The most sensation comes from where visitors are generally sitting, on the lower deck two rearside seats. Putting them there also means that when the bus stops, they often get soaked by the water spraying jets, which just happen to be aimed that way.

Actually for that demonstration, the pupil does very little, (apart from pray). He is told to drive on to the pad at speed, and when instructed, come off the gas, take both hands off the wheel and put them down by his side, almost sitting on them. The instructor leans over him, grabs the wheel in one hand, applies a bit of lock, then the handbrake with the other hand, then with both hands puts on more lock and the bus spins.

The first run was as described above, with a dramatic spin, following that, the serious bit. No problem there, I understood brake pumping very well, as on my early Mini, the only way to get decent brakes was to pump them. After a few runs I managed to achieve a reasonable result.

Admittedly a poor quality photo, but the only one I know of showing an experimental livery carried by RMC 1469 for a time. *Author*

But to finish off he said he would like me to go round a lot faster, which I did, and on the approach the devil reached through over my shoulders, grabbed the steering wheel and the handbrake, got the bus going in a sideways skid, "Sort that out, and stop in the box." Good fun in a way, so I asked if I might be shown how to spin the bus, just like in the demonstrations.

That fun happened the next Friday afternoon, when things were quiet and I hadn't been to the pub. I was shown the rudiments of the deliberate skid, and then allowed under supervision to practise it, managing to get the bus right round and facing the direction that we had entered by. At the end of the session, when walking toward the training building, I was congratulated by some American visitors on "How good you Instructors are." My reply of "I'm not an Instructor Sir, I'm the works electronics engineer," seemed to mystify them.

It was not uncommon for visitors to be allowed to drive a bus on the skid, so I asked if my son, who was nearing eighteen and had recently passed his car test, could have a go. We arrived at about 9.30 on the next Saturday and found our friendly instructor. Following a few introductions I left Barrie with him, whilst I did some odd work in my office. After about an hour he hadn't returned, so I went to find him.

The instructor had not only shown him skid control, but had also let him drive RM 1740 around the roads of the Chiswick site, passing on some useful tips about driving in general. Leaving the bus, I thanked him profusely for his kindness, and he responded by saying that he wished that he had more pupils that good. Exit from the works, one very happy son.

This view, taken from the front nearside seat of an RM, shows what confronted a driver on the approach to the skid pad. Clearly on the right are the water sprays, and the puddles formed. On the road in the middle distance, you can just about see the yellow markings, where you should end up. On no account should you end up in the training building, which is immediately in front! *Author*

A further investigation I got involved in was at Sidcup garage, which had a Titan fitted experimentally with a Voith gearbox in place of a Leyland one. The reported problem was that it would not go into 3rd gear until the bus was doing 38mph. Normally the change from 2nd to 3rd happened around 28–30mph. Sitting in the canteen at Sidcup waiting for the bus to come in off service (yes, they were still using it), Mike (from electrical development) and I calculated that the engine must really be super, as to do 38mph in 2nd gear meant it must be doing over 2,500rpm, instead of the normal maximum of around 1,900. Mike drove the bus and I followed in the car, and he waved out of the window when it changed – 29mph on the car speedo. It transpired that someone had removed the gearbox converter drive from the top of the gearbox. This little box contained a reduction gear-set that interfaced the differential ratio with the type of speedo. The reason for the removal was that the other Titans didn't have one, and they thought it a mistake. Anyway putting it back cured the apparent fault!

The approval to drive buses came in very useful one night going home, when our dear RMA decided to fail on Barnes Common, and it didn't help that it happened one night when Tony was on holiday, so Mick was on his own.

RMs are fitted with several alternator belts, and all except one had gone, and that was so loose it was not doing anything – so much for maintenance. Mick decided that turning it over (and we had no tools) should effectively shorten the belt and give enough tension to allow it to grip, and that's what he tried. But what a messy job. He emerged from under the bus covered in grease saying he had done it, and would I get up in the cab and start it up. All was well, but Mick was too dirty to drive, so he asked if I would drive, as far as Tadworth anyway; no-one else on the bus was vehicle approved. This I agreed to do and it caused some great amusement from the factory workers, here being driven home by a section engineer. I didn't mind.

The bus had a very smooth gearbox, where the driver could push the lever directly from one gear to the next and just relax the throttle a tiny bit when doing so; this was the technique I had watched Tony and Mick use, so I just copied it. I did manage just under 60 mph along the A3, not as fast as Mick or Tony, but enough for me.

We had RMA 36 for most of the time, it only being subbed when away for maintenance, which from what I remember was done by Norbiton or Stamford Brook. On those occasions we had various buses, generally borrowed from the training school: a Metro, an LS or even a standard Routemaster.

It was a few days after one such return of our bus that it failed on an inward journey; we ran out of fuel at Belmont. Sutton garage very kindly came to the rescue, and off we went, but our drivers could not understand it, usually a full tank would last a certain number of days. The problem was then diagnosed. Apparently RMAs had a larger fuel tank than standard RMs and when in for service, because corrosion was noticed on our tank, it was decided to change it, but the only ones the garage had were standard ones and that's what they fitted. Wish they had told us!

Then one day we noticed excessive vibration and banging over bumps and a definite lean to one side. Inspection showed problems with the mounting on the rear sub-frame around the air bag support areas. It was deemed too expensive to repair, so the bus got condemned.

Our replacements varied; RMA 50 was still in blue and white from its airport days, but now had a red bonnet fitted. My memory fails (again), but I think we had RMA 16 as the regular after that, but whatever it was, it had a standard bus differential, which meant the top speed was around 42mph, certainly not enough for the Reigate Staff Bus.

To cure this, one lunch hour Tony and Mick set about swapping the differentials between RMAs 36 and 16, but then the bus had no guts because of the higher ratio back axle. So next day it was off with the fuel pump and into the pump shop with it for a slight tweak!. That night we were back in business – no one beats the Reigate Staff Bus. It's a shame I wasn't there about five years earlier, when I believe the vehicle was a GS!

This restored CDS lorry 580 EYU often made appearances in the works. *Author*

Bill the type trainer had become a good friend, and every so often would come and say that I had not been out for a while, and we should go for a short drive. What he really meant was that he needed to go to Greenford, or some place to collect something. But it worked both ways.

Some months earlier I had bought a video recorder, which had an ongoing fault of wavering sound, and I had on two previous occasions struggled on a bus up to the shop, just off the A40 at Northolt by the Target pub. I need some more type training I told myself, and asked if Bill would give me a refresher in a Titan. Parking the bus was no problem as there was a bus stop just outside the shop.

Inside the shop the service personnel were as helpful, or less, as on previous occasions, saying there was nothing wrong with the machine, but on listening to it in the shop it was obvious that all was not well. Then from behind me came this almost bellowing voice with a German accent. "I zink there is somezing wrong, you vill fix it." That, and the big black coat, must have frightened the life out of them, as they immediately offered to return the machine to Grundig for attention, who actually a week later exchanged it for another.

Aldenham was still a going concern with a bus going there from Chiswick first thing every morning and returning mid-afternoon; the usual vehicle being RMA 1. They also had a vast number of staff buses still running, and it was said that it was a spectacle to see them all charging down the A41 three abreast towards Edgware to see who could get to the roundabout first. I didn't often go there, but one of my radio men often went to maintain their wardens' radio system.

Life continued at a steady pace, even though "things were happening". Chiswick was still working to principles born many years back when materials were difficult to obtain but labour was easier.

Using this philosophy, worn out components were by various means remanufactured into as good as new condition. With mechanical parts, this was usually achieved by metal spraying or electro-plating to build up a layer of new material and then careful machining to the required size. Motors were often rewound by hand.

It was becoming apparent that these were costly exercises, and that often the item could be replaced by new at a fraction of the re-manufacturing cost. So various exercises were introduced to identify components where this applied, and this played a big factor in the remodelling of both of the overhaul works.

On the horizon was the proposal to close Aldenham Works, mainly brought about by the change in overhaul methods for the newer vehicles necessitated by their design, and also by the fact that garages were doing more of their own repairs to the RM fleet.

It was not possible to dismantle into various components the classes like DMs. Story has it that a pilot programme was set up, which included separating a body from the chassis, but when the body was stood up, it fell over, according to the description I heard, like "a pack of cards".

Various viable sections of Aldenham eventually transferred to Chiswick, and this was completed on 15th November 1986. The building in the centre by the top of the Dip that was previously the plant department was turned into a vehicle overhaul shop, looking rather like Aldenham, and though very much smaller, similar work was done there. Destination blinds and a smaller trim shop were also transferred, and they occupied a small area in the main works building. The ticket machine works from Effra Road Brixton also appeared, originally going into a small section vacated by personnel, who moved to the block by the Bollo Road entrance.

To allow the original big canteen to be vacated and hence release the front part of the site for sale, a new and much smaller canteen was built in a section previously partly occupied by stationery supplies and distribution services. It was opened on 20th October 1986 and was christened 'Wheels'. To advertise this, on the first day all lunches were free, so we all went, but it was never very popular and closed after a short while.

Proof that quality did not suffer after the closure of Aldenham. Prior to a re-paint, RM 529 is undergoing heavy preparation at the new Chiswick facility. *Author*

LONDON REGIONAL TRANSPORT'S BUS ENGINEERING LTD

The London Transport bus business was now divided into two. The overhaul/repair sections were separated from the bus operating division, which became known as London Buses Limited (LBL).

What really made a difference to us, was the setting up on 1st April 1985 of Bus Engineering Ltd (BEL), a wholly owned subsidiary of London Regional Transport (LRT). In my view this was the best set-up we had. We had in effect the protection of LRT but being a subsidiary company we were allowed to go out and get business from wherever, and that we did. A dedicated sales team was set up, which included all the necessary support for such an enterprise. Several of the middle managers with a flair for sales were given a bit of training and became sales representatives. To help promote the services available, sales stands were taken at many trade fairs. There was so much enthusiasm from all involved.

As I had worked previously as a sales representative, I had some idea of the requirements. One of the new reps who became a good friend was Bob McConnell. Bob was an ex-AEC man and had had a big influence in the engine rebuild shop, so he knew engines very well. Bob and I often went out to see customers, where I dealt with electrical items, and Bob the mechanical. Customers liked him because he knew the subjects well and could talk about their problems, and as he originally hailed from Ireland had that built-in humour also.

A product we became aware of from visiting potential customers was an

Just out of the paint shop on 8th July 1985, RMA 16 exhibits an experimental colour just after the setting up of LRT BEL. *Author*

electronic 'Translator Panel' used with semi automatic gearboxes, known as an LVS 45. These in various guises were often used on Olympians, Nationals, Tiger coaches, VRTs and basically anything that had a semi-automatic box. Their purpose was to inhibit gear availability under certain conditions. From standstill the top two gears of a five speed transmission were inhibited, so if you tried to pull away in one of those you got neutral. This feature also had its advantages, in that when you pulled up with 4th or 5th still selected, when stationary you automatically got neutral, which stopped you idling in gear, but you needed to remember to apply the hand-brake. Possibly its main use was over-speed protection, in that if travelling at speed, for example in 5th at about 40mph, if you selected 2nd as some idiot drivers were known to do, the gear stayed in 5th until the road speed was reduced to be appropriate for the next lower gear, so it went to 4th, then 3rd then 2nd as you slowed down. Also provided was reverse-forward interlock – if while going forward reverse was selected, you didn't get it until you stopped, likewise the other way.

With a view to obtaining circuit details, I made contact with the company that had originally manufactured these panels, only to be told it had been sold on when the holding company was divided up. At first the new company weren't terribly helpful, as the product was new and unknown to them, and did not fit in with their present product structure. So I bluntly asked if they would like us to become a sub-contractor as it was our business. Following several meetings with their managing director, the whole repair franchise was sold to us along with a vast number of useful spares on 28th September 1987. Also passed over was a customer list with contact names, to whom I immediately wrote introducing our company and what we had to offer. The work flooded in. Let's face it, who in the bus world hadn't heard of Chiswick Works?

But the LVS product was not as well mechanically engineered or electronically designed as the automatic version (LVA). And on some of the examples sent in for repair, various attempts had been made to improve the reliability, with some having very dubious re-designs. In fact, many went against the first principles of electronics and actually made matters worse.

Following some experience we decided that apart from the actual repairing of the fault, all panels would have a standard upgrade procedure to parts that we believed would improve it, and also stop premature failures.

I got wind that the main canteen was about to be flattened, and I knew that there were some big loudspeakers on the wall there, which were used on the occasions when dances were held. These would be very useful in our village hall I thought, so enquiries were made into how I might buy the two smallest ones. The person in charge of site demolition agreed to sell me the two for £10, so the £10 was paid, a receipt given and I was told to go and see the foreman who would remove them from the wall for you. "Come back in an hour," he said, and when I did so said that I might as well have all the others as well – he had cleared it with the manager. Trouble was that these six others were much bigger than my originally requested ones, so how was I going to get them home? Wally came up with the answer.

"We've got to road test that experimental M 597 with the Maxwell gear box that has just been modified." Permission was granted, I won't say from whom, but we loaded up the bus and drove it along the old 406 route from Kingston to Tadworth.

This test route goes back many years, and was used because of its varying terrains. For fuel usage measurement tests, the test vehicle followed behind a normal service bus, and tried to replicate what it did. Going back, another reason to use the 406 could have been because it was operated by Reigate garage, the headquarters of Country Bus Engineering. Remember the tests of RM 2 on the 406? I do, but only because I lived nearby and took what turned out to be some very tatty photos with my mother's box camera.

M 597 was going well until the top of Ashley Road approaching the Downs, when just like the RTs used to on a hot day, it expired – but luckily only temporarily. The gearbox was overheating due to the steepish hill. After a short rest all was OK and off we went, eventually parking it on the grass verge outside my house.

When my wife looked through the window and saw Wally and me and a big red bus, she said to herself, "What are those two up to now?" Returning to Chiswick was uneventful, but I reported the overheat problem, which turned out to be a clogged heat exchanger. "Good job you found it," I was told, "tomorrow it was planned to go out on the 91."

A Gibson ticket machine dismantled for reconditioning. *Author*

A staff bus we sometimes used, was RMA 50 still in blue and white, but sporting a red bonnet. Seen here in October 1984. *Author*

A mixture of staff RMAs, showing how after the setting up of BEL, some were painted grey. *Author*

The 'borrowing' of test buses for personal use was frowned upon, but still went on. I remember one morning seeing a DMS parked outside Argos in Chiswick High Road, with its engine cover raised and a seat propped against the rear, the intention being to suggest to a traffic warden that it had failed. There was an occasion however when the borrower returned with his shopping to find out that it had, and following an embarrassing phone call the boys walked down to fix a faulty micro switch on an engine door cover.

BOUGHT OUT BY FRONTSOURCE

It became obvious that the setting up of a subsidiary company, had been in preparation for the sale of LRT's Bus Engineering Ltd to the private sector, and this eventually happened on 13th January 1988 with the sale to Frontsource.

Suddenly our unit manager, Vic Osborne, was no more, he just seemed to vanish. There was no handover to the new Frontsource Management which appeared only to be the director, Shon Laird, a Scotsman, who was an accountant with no engineering experience.

Initially we just got on with running our own sections, which in some cases were reduced in size. The main electrical shop had effectively closed, with work on alternators, starters, hydraulics, fuel injection and air components being contracted out. But in their place there was a new paint facility, partly using the area that was previously the pump shop.

Frontsource was owned by a Mr Beattie, and at first it looked as though big things would happen. Amongst his other concerns, he had also bought Southdown Engineering at Portslade, United Counties at Northampton, Eastern National Engineering at Chelmsford, Bristol Engineering and later on, the London Country overhaul works at Crawley.

I personally had a discussion with Shon Laird, wherein he said that because of our unique knowledge of bus electronics, "the subject of the future", all bus electronic work would be sent to Chiswick. Initially this didn't account for much, because the other establishments who had little knowledge of the subject were doing very little, but to be fair after I went and spoke to Bristol and Southdown, they considered electronics could be added to their product list, and should be offered to their existing customer base. Then work did start to come in. Frontsource wanted to concentrate all the business on the area of Chiswick works by the Bollo Lane end, and so we moved out of the Portakabins and into the building previously inhabited by Road Services and latterly by our personnel. Next door was the new canteen, which by then had closed.

Moving of the radio/electronics shops was achieved by many journeys along the road at the side of the 'Dip' – using a flat bedded trolley borrowed from the main works. Thinking we had finished our move, we had just sat down for a cuppa, when Shon appeared with the news that there were still three buses parked on the skid patch area, and could I help with their

RT 1 arrives at Chiswick in April 1989, fifty years after it was built there, carrying specially-made blinds welcoming it back. *Author*

removal. Like a shot I was out to get one, probably one of the last to be driven across 'The Pad', a red RMC. The area was then fenced off and the work of demolition began.

However, the road alongside the top of the Dip to where our old Portakabins were was still accessible, and it was about this time that RT 1 was on site for a re-paint. My task for that duration was to drive it up and down this stretch of road for about half an hour every other day, just "to keep it going". The top deck of the bus was a useful grandstand allowing me to take photos of the site being demolished.

Because of falling passenger numbers, the RMA staff buses had been disposed of and replaced by three Leyland Sherpa Minibuses, but that was a short term agreement and when it finished we were left to our own devices of how to get to work. The only vehicle access into the site became the Bollo Lane one, and I don't remember the Sherpas ever leaving by that so their withdrawal must have been some considerable time earlier. Of the original drivers, Tony Elmer had taken a position as a mechanical instructor at a garage and I believe Mick Dark had taken redundancy.

Our new driver was Mick Bell, and the normal overnight parking place for the bus had been changed from Reigate garage to a place close to his house. I do remember that over a Christmas break when he was away on holiday I took charge of it and parked it in the car park adjacent to my property.

The repair of both LVA and LVS45 control panels was really taking off, with work coming in from far and wide; our good reputation was spreading quickly within the industry. One such repair concerned a fully automatic Olympian which had been admitted to the factory for an engine re-fit plus an investigation into an alleged gear control panel fault.

On return of the bus to the owner in Chelmsford the owner complained that it kept on losing its gears, and in view of the amount of money paid for the supposed repair, insisted that we visited his premises to diagnose the problem. I decided that Wally should accompany me; so along with a spare control panel and a 'loom checker' we travelled by train to Chelmsford. Unfortunately changing the control panel did nothing to cure the faults, which were that either it would not change up out of the starting gear or if it did, in a random fashion the gear box would sequence into 5th gear. With the facilities on offer, this was not to going to be an 'easy fix'. The only option was to return the bus to Chiswick for fuller investigation.

The loom checker came into use here, but not in a way that it was intended. The loom checker is really just a continuity checker that plugs into the bus loom in place of the control panel. It applies a voltage to the loom which energises the hydracyclic valve which in turn gives that gear. The total current taken by the series combination of hydracyclic valve and cable assembly is displayed on a meter. The gear you wish to check is selected via a rotary switch on the checker.

It was decided to connect this apparatus, and with me driving the bus I

Probably the most remembered occurrence at Chiswick before its demise was the preparation of the Routemasters for export to Colombo, Sri Lanka. The most obvious modification to the buses was the replacement of the standard drop light windows by full height side-sliding ones.

would shout instructions to Wally relating to the gear I wanted, and he would turn the selector knob accordingly. On this Olympian the control panel was mounted behind a panel at the top of the stairs, so for the long journey, he removed a seat cushion to sit on. We made very good progress, as a good percentage of the journey is on an open road where no gear changes were necessary. On each pull-away I would shout instructions like "2nd gear," then as our speed increased "3rd," then "4th" and "5th." We were a good team and arrived back at Chiswick in the late afternoon.

Next day we diagnosed the fault, which turned out to be poor and erratic output from the perception head; a magnetic transducer that reads the rotational speed of a toothed wheel mounted on the output shaft of the gearbox and produces a voltage relative to that speed. From this the speed of the bus is determined.

Removing the end cover of the gearbox revealed that although the toothed wheel was tightly fitted to the shaft and therefore not slipping, the shaft had an end float movement of such a degree that it was allowing the toothed wheel to go completely out of alignment with the transducer. This would produce an erratic output from the transducer and cause the panel to behave in the same erratic fashion. A costly gearbox rebuild was needed, with which the customer was none too happy as it was not related to any previous work we had undertaken, but he accepted it. He was very lucky the gearbox didn't completely fail on the road. The bus was returned with a perfect transmission system about a week later.

Rear yard at Willesden, with evidence of several BLs and some Titans. *Author*

UNDER YET ANOTHER OWNERSHIP

The Frontsource business didn't last very long. According to records it went into receivership sometime in 1989, and an internal news-sheet I have says it was sold in 1991 to Bus Engineering Group, a company with Tony Cook as the chairman and Shon Laird as a director. This soon went into receivership and was sold to Shon Laird who kept the name B.E.L. with the full stops added to distinguish it from the previous set-up. In all the moves and takeovers, there are discrepancies between the dates on the newsletters we were given and those now available from Companies House.

The locations of the new smaller layout didn't last long. The new site owners wanted us off the Chiswick site quickly, and I believe B.E.L. gained a bonus if they did so. Records show that the BEL lease for the Chiswick site expired end September 1989, so there must have been a new short lease with the new owners. What was thought to be a suitably sized site was found in Salter Street, a small road at the end of Hythe Road, which itself was a turning off Scrubs Lane near Willesden Junction.

Hythe Road had two railway bridges along it, both of which raised some concern. However Shon Laird assured us that at some time the road had been lowered and although there was a very steep entrance and exit at the bridges, it was possible to get high vehicles through. We were not convinced, so a trip was organised with an RML to prove it. He was right, there was adequate clearance even for a much longer vehicle.

The new site consisted of two large, relatively new hangar-style buildings, and apart from a small area over the front where there was some office accommodation, were both single storey. At the rear was an area with room for some bus parking. Unfortunately I have not been able to find confirmation of the exact date we moved.

We did a lot of the move ourselves, and the radio and electronics sections were initially 'dumped' in a small corner at the front of the left hand building. Somehow during all this upheaval we still managed to deal with the increasing amount of electronics work, but luckily the radio business was dropping off, because 'Band 3' radio was now being fitted to the buses and that was still under warranty and maintained by the supplier.

It soon became apparent that the building as it stood was sadly lacking in space, and the answer was to add a mezzanine floor in one of the buildings. The chosen location was almost immediately above where our area was currently located, which meant that during the construction we were subjected to vast amounts of dust, banging and all the nuisance of a building site. The main stores was to be located under the mezzanine floor and we were to be located above it. This was the final move for the radio/electronics workshop.

Within the main stores was a 'special' cupboard, where under lock and key, all the useful domestic items that may easily 'go walkies' were kept; things like paint brushes and superglue to name but a few. The 'special' feature of this cupboard was that although fitted with a very expensive padlock on the door, it had no back, so all of the contents could easily be accessed by reaching through from the row behind!

Being on the top floor where at the edges the curved roof was a trifle low gave the setting a slightly claustrophobic feel, and in the hot summer it was like a sauna. For the cold winter we managed to "obtain" some blow heaters. The electronics shop only occupied a small area, the remainder being taken up with what was left of the blind shop, the trim shop and the ticket machine works. Before his retirement, George Sawyer, who was the manager when it was situated at Effra Road Brixton, occupied a lot of his time by assisting with the repair of the Gibsons. George and his men were experts on the Gibson ticket machine, which unfortunately was being rapidly replaced by the Wayfarer electronic machine. There was still a high throughput of Gibson machines because they were being prepared for sale at the London Transport Museum. From further afield there was a customer from Kano in Nigeria who bought 150 reconditioned Gibsons.

Part of the preparation included the compulsory removal of the London Transport insignia from the drum, and this was done with a small hand grinder, but first the access hole was covered with a damp cloth to stop the swarf from entering the works.

The bus routes being run on behalf of LRT all had Wayfarer machines, and only these were repaired by the works at Willesden; all those being fitted on LBL buses were maintained by Wayfarer. Most repairs related to failed keyboards, drive motors or displays and were executed, by replacing faulty complete circuit boards supplied by Wayfarer, as the section did not have the expertise or equipment to do board repairs.

Wayfarers worked on the module principle, i.e. the machine was a permanent fixture on the bus and had a slot for a removable module, which was issued to the driver at the start of duty. This module stored all the transactions, along with various other data during the tour of duty, which was downloaded to a 'Depot Reader' at the end of duty. Obviously included in this download was how much money had to be handed in. One thing we knew how to do, and it was the best kept secret ever, was how to erase this information. Imagine a driver being able to just hand in £10.00 for a day, when it should have been £30.00.

Soon George said it was time for him to retire and I was given the jobs of managing ticket machine repair and the blind shop and the trim shop. In all, I was responsible for a staff of about fourteen.

The blind shop was by then only doing small special paper inserts, but the trim shop had quite a lucrative business still, both with London Buses and the many small companies that were cropping up, and for these we had a vast selection of different colours and styles of moquette. Through the efforts of the salesmen, the trim shop widened its customer base, and tackled jobs like seat repairs for clubs and theatres. All trim shop personnel were ex-Aldenham, and were extremely clever and versatile in their work. I had great admiration for their expertise.

I mentioned one day that I had just acquired a new dog and needed to buy a bed for him. Later on a bed appeared, the inside being fabricated from stiff foam, the outer covering in standard Routemaster moquette. At the time, I wondered as to the reason for this present, and whether it had any relation to an incident a week or two earlier. Returning from lunch one day, I noticed that three of the trimmers were missing from their benches, but I could hear their voices in the rear of their stores. And there they were, working on a beautiful three-piece settee, partly recovered with what looked like a very expensive piece of material. Various reasons emerged regarding them overrunning their dinner break, but I didn't really care, they were a good bunch, so I just said "Keep your voices down," and walked away.

I shudder to think what would have been the reaction if Shon Laird, the managing director had found them. Going way back, when he first appeared on the scene, even considering his lack of engineering knowledge, I had a reasonably high respect for him, especially as soon after his appointment he invited all of his managers to a barbecue at his house, so that he could get to know them. Shon was a single man and had arranged a cook for the occasion. Like my wife, he had an interest in art and had many paintings hung around his house. He got great pleasure from her interest, and was more than pleased to show her around. Later on she asked me if he ever did any dirty work as she had never seen such clean hands!

The contract for the repair of Wayfarer ticket machines included us sending a man to the various operators' sites such as Len Wright's or London Country at Hatfield. The intention was to try to correct the faults on site, and if not they were brought back to the works for repair. The mid-morning tea break was staggered throughout the works and ticket machine staff took theirs at 10.15. At 11.00, Shon came into my office and reported that one of my staff was still having tea, and when he asked him why, said he would not reply without me being present. I explained that he was the roving engineer and had only just returned, and therefore missed the start of his allocated break. Unfortunately to Shon it didn't seem to have any bearing on the case; the subject was not open to discussion. After Shon had gone, I said to the driver, "In future just find someplace to have your break away from his eyes, like on the road somewhere, and take your time about it."

The latest "flavour of the month" in the transport industry was the fitting of 'Bus Stopping' signs. These displayed 'Bus Stopping' on a panel in the lower saloon only, and were to inform passengers that a request to stop at the next stop had been already made, so there was no need to repeat the bell push. We were fortunate to win a contract to fit some London Buses' Metros with these, and it was my job to oversee the electrical work.

Not a big job; a relay was energised by a pulse from the bell push circuit. This relay used its own second set of contacts to hold itself on. At a bus stop the display cancelled when the relay received a signal from the push button that opened the centre exit doors. All that the wiring entailed was threading three pairs of wires from the cab area to a terminal box halfway down the bus, and because these wires were all the same type and colour, they were supposed to have identification labels fitted to both ends prior to pulling them through.

Many weeks went by without a hitch, when suddenly a plea was received from the vehicle shop for Wally to go down and assist, as they couldn't get one to work. About half an hour later Wally returned scratching his head, saying all was wired up correctly, the relay was OK but nothing worked.

Donning my scruffy coat I accompanied Wally to the bus, where we completely removed all the new cables, and there emerged the fault. The same cable had ident 'A' on one end, and ident 'B' on the other end.

When I later questioned the mechanical fitter on the team, he said the electrical fitter had pulled all the wires through, but without fitting the identification tags, and then proceeded to connect the cables as well as he could. In the end he fitted the idents incorrectly.

Another problem occurred when someone reported that it looked as if the plastic case of a sign was melting. Investigation showed it wasn't, but it was well on the way. What some fool had done was fit the unit with bulbs of a much higher wattage, and these of course do produce rather more heat.

In reminiscing these occurrences to the great late Bill Cottrell, foreman of Holloway garage, he said that the only claim one of his electricians had to being an electrician was the fact that he used to drive an electric milk float!

As the throughput of work increased, so did my need to go out to correct faulty workmanship done in our own repair shops. One instance was to an Atlantean we had done for London Country at Grays. The reported fault was that the bell would sound as the bus was switched on; but none of the bell pushes would cause it to sound. The work on this bus had included the removal of the centre vertical poles in the lower saloon. But whoever replaced them used different screws that were much, much longer than the ones taken out, with the result that they went through the wiring loom which runs between the decks. The short circuit produced caused the bell solenoid to remain energised and kept the hammer hard against the bell cover, so it couldn't go back ready for the next strike.

The other visit to London Country of any scale was a complaint that one of our recently repaired LVS gear panels failed after about 10 minutes, whereupon no gears were available. Off I went to Hertford and duly fitted another panel to the vehicle in question, a Tiger coach. Then along with the garage manager, we were driven on a test run by a fitter. And guess what? Yes, it also failed, or rather appeared to. "Have you checked over the bus," I asked, "like the oil levels in the gearbox and flywheel?" Suddenly something must have clicked in their heads, as they stared blankly at each other. Please check them now I asked. The flywheel oil level was as I suspected low, not just low, but very low, too low to allow the flywheel to lock up and give 'drive'. After a short while of operation the oil fills up all the crevices, filters, etc., the level drops and produces this condition.

The method of checking oil level in most automatic transmissions of that type is to start up the engine, put it in and out of gear a couple of times, switch off and then immediately check the level. If you just check the oil after the bus has been stationary for some time, a quantity of the oil has run back from the flywheel to the gearbox sump and will give a higher reading, which can be construed as being acceptable. And in our case I bet that's what had happened, because when we finally got back to the garage and added more in the way described, on the second test trip it was perfect.

By the way, the method for recovering a vehicle fitted with a Hydracyclic gearbox that fails is to manually wind in the second speed solenoid. It's a horrible job, especially on a Titan, and you usually end up with smelly oil up your arm. And you need to be careful, as it can be hot.

I had often admired the London Country LRC class: superior looking Green Line double deckers, coach seats, carpets and all the trimmings, supposedly an upmarket Olympian. The chance to drive one at Northfleet after I had refitted a gear control panel deadened this admiration.

There I was, expecting a bus with a 'bit of go' for Green Line work, but what a disappointment. It was gutless, sloppy, and the general feel of the bus was not good. Maybe it was just this example, and I was unlucky; I never did get a drive of another one.

During these visits to other companies it was quite normal for me to drive their buses, and without any type training from them. I asked some local drivers about this, and they said that because they had so many variants, often only one example, that it was nigh on impossible to be type trained on everything. "You get used to muddling through," they told me.

There was an occasion concerning what was, I believe, an ex Northern General front-entrance Routemaster. Simple, all Routemasters are the same. Wrong. I couldn't get the engine to turn over; it had a different start routine which somehow involved the positions of some switches up next to the normal engine start switch, which itself had been put on a key. Not wanting to advertise publicly what a fool I was, I played with various options until it started.

Westlink were a good customer of both our electronics shop for gear panels and the mechanical shops for engine changes etc. They had a fair collection of Leyland Nationals, but their engineering manager, Gary Filby, didn't like the standard settings, saying that they went into some gears at the wrong speed and with a jolt. So we set about doing some actual road tests, whereby, with some adjustments we arrived at what he wanted. The gear panel was then removed, and taken back to the workshop, where we put it on the test gear and measured the parameters. From that day, all future Westlink repairs were set to these parameters. This method is sometimes known as 'reverse engineering'.

The old Kingston bus garage was by now under the control of Westlink, and the story goes that late one night, a manager found a not too dirty or smelly tramp asleep on one of the buses, and when questioned said he had nowhere to go. Instead of turning him out, the manager said he could stay, but he had to do a job, and promptly gave him a broom and told him to sweep out some of the buses. The story concludes by saying that he was so good at it, he was actually around for some weeks and was even paid a few quid out of petty cash.

There are two other occurrences concerning Westlink that come to mind, and both involved Titans. A bus had been sent to our works for an engine change, which was completed without too much problem, except that in the rush no-one had ordered new water hoses for the cooling system. It is a well known engineering fact, that once hoses have been in position for many years they become hard. When re-using a hose in this condition if the securing clip is not seated in the same groove made by the original clip then a leak can occur, and on inspection this was apparent on this bus. The annoying thing was that the fitter was quite prepared to return the bus in this state, saying that they wanted it back quickly and he would deal with it "in a few days". For a "few days" read "never". Wally and I weren't happy about this sloppy workmanship going back to one of the electronics shop's good customers, plus which it could run out of water and cause the engine to seize and result in a warranty claim against the company.

Actually Titans and Metros had a device called an 'Engine Protection Unit' which monitored water level and would shut down the engine if it was too low. But many drivers knew that if they changed over two connectors on the unit, it would disengage the circuit. That knowledge was useful if the bus failed in the middle of heavy traffic, but was often abused.

What did Wally do? He put a fault on the gear system, which no-one else understood, then said the part would take about a day to fix, during which there was time to change the hoses. The hoses did get changed, and in no time at all a miracle cure was performed on the gear system.

The next occurrence at Westlink concerned a gear control panel on a Titan that they had fitted themselves. It was one that we had just repaired, and like so many, had excessive corrosion on the circuit board and a terrible smell when the top of the panel was removed. Both these were from the same source. It seemed a normal thing that if drivers were 'caught short' late at night and had no immediate facility, they would urinate in the windscreen reservoir, and when they missed, their discharge went over the gear control panel, then collected in the inspection glass, which, as it didn't have a very good seal, eventually found its way to the electronics within.

The message on the phone said that the bus would not give top (5th) gear until it was warmed up. So off to Kingston Wally and I went, armed with a spare panel. It was often customary for me to attend supposed warranty claims, just in case there was a problem. Out of Kingston Garage we went, then sharp right around the one way system, past Norbiton Garage and up

A BL similar to the ones we modified was BL 81, allocated to Westlink at Hounslow. It received a full Westlink livery and retained the high backed coach style seats. *Author*

Kingston Hill towards the A3. The bus was not making very good progress and appeared to be lumbering a lot; and true, even on the flat it wouldn't go into 5th. We found a place to turn on the A3 and retraced our steps back to Kingston down the hill, when hey!, we've got 5th. There are no prizes for why. It was obvious from the outset that the engine was gutless and was incapable of moving the bus fast enough on a flat road to the road speed required for 5th gear.

Back at the garage, sitting in the cab discussing the problem with the bus in neutral, I revved it up, and to me it was not going to maximum revs. Lifting the engine cover and looking at the throttle linkage revealed the problem; there was a huge gap between the maximum throttle stop and the throttle actuating arm – the engine was not getting full throttle.

Enter Wally with his two metric adjustable spanners; adjust throttle rods in accordance with the method stated in the Leyland service manual, and we had a bus that went like a rocket and got 5th on the flat. Exit a rather embarrassed engineering manager.

The worst thing about Westlink was their Pulborough Way site at Hounslow Heath, near Heathrow Airport. Planes flew over there so low you could almost see the occupants. The noise was ear splitting if you were in the yard, but the best thing about Westlink was that, for a while anyway, they owned RT 1530, and BEL had been commissioned to repaint it. BEL did quite a few repaints of preserved buses. One of them, RCL 2254, was done in a BEL advert livery but actually was privately owned, and was partially fitted out as a hospitality suite.

It was during the preparation of the RT that a huge explosion occurred on it. Like many buses that are not frequently used, the batteries had gone flat, so it was being jump started from the battery booster trolley. This was just a set of batteries on a trolley and for safety, had a big on/off switch on it. After the RT was started using assistance from the trolley, at the RT end one of the battery crocodile clips was just pulled off, but without switching off the supply from the trolley. Unfortunately the electrician dropped the clip he had just removed, and it fell on to the RT battery, which was the type with exposed links joining the cells on the top. As luck didn't have it, it fell across the first link, i.e. one cell, where the nominal voltage is only about 2.2 volts. The voltage being applied to it from the trolley was around 24, and the resulting current flow into the single cell was too much for it, so it exploded. The only injury apart from the battery, was to the electrician's head as he tried to emerge quickly from the RT battery compartment, which is under the stairs. In doing so, he banged his head on the surround and a big cut ensued. He was extremely lucky not to have had battery acid sprayed over him. There was another battery explosion on another occasion, but this time the other equipment involved was a very quick boost charger. This device gave a very high output and would supposedly charge up a flat battery in a very short time. The Titan in question was being treated to this procedure.

Above preserved RTW 467 being prepared for repaint at the Willesden site of BEL. RCL 2254 is alongside. And below just out of the paint shop and without transfers. *Author*

When the electrician thought it had had enough, and without switching off the charger, he just pulled off one of the crocodile clips, and bang, the top of the battery blew off; it hit the top of the battery inspection door and then hit him in the face.

When batteries are being charged in that manner they discharge gas at a high rate and all that's needed is some ignition. A nice spark will do; and this conveniently happened when the crocodile clip was pulled off with a high current flowing. And hey presto!, you have your very own explosion. Again he was very lucky, and I do believe it was the same electrician.

Kevin was an addition to the sales team as a technical salesman. He was a very versatile salesman and had a vast experience of unit overhaul and also a huge love of railways and modelling them. I accompanied Kevin on many customer visits and on one such, to South Wales Transport (SWT) in Swansea, we became diverted on the return journey and ended up at Barry Island where there was once a huge collection of withdrawn steam locomotives awaiting scrapping. Unfortunately by the time we got there, very little remained.

Southampton City Bus was a company exploited by Kevin with a little help from me as a potential buyer of spare parts for their fleet of recently acquired Routemasters.

How misled you can be by a voice on the phone; you image what the face and person must be like. For some while I had been dealing with a small company based in the West Midlands who themselves repaired various electrical components but sub-contracted all their electronic work to us. My contact had an accent normal for that location. I decided that to thank him for all the work, a personal visit was called for and duly organised a mutual time. Image my surprise, when in the reception of the company I was greeted by this very large gentleman with very dark skin and supporting a turban. Over lunch he confided that he only wore the turban in respect for his father, saying that when father died he would remove it, as he believed it was hampering his personal commercial progress, and after all this is England! The last comment I was very surprised to hear.

A lovely day out could be had going to visit the Southern Vectis company on the Isle of Wight.

I usually visited them when there was a gear panel or two (but no more because they were heavy) to be returned after repair, and it was more of a goodwill visit and thanking them for the business. The gear panels were of the semi-automatic protection type and fitted their Olympians.

To get to the Island, I usually started the journey directly from my house early in the morning, having taken all the material home the night before. The route started with my wife driving me to Reigate, where I caught a train to Guildford and changed to another, usually a 4CEP, to Portsmouth Harbour where it seemed impossible for the train operator (BR) and the hydrofoil company to make their connections coincide, so often a long wait ensued.

After concluding my business I usually walked back to the bus station in Newport and in the café there had some lunch, where if I chose the right table, could also watch the movement of buses. If I got back to the mainland around 15.00, I would catch the once a day diesel hauled, InterCity Service from Portsmouth Harbour, which went via Guildford and then the Reading route to the Midlands. This train had superior coaching stock to the SR EMUs and was hauled into Portsmouth station by a little 08 diesel shunter.

On one occasion when arriving at Portsmouth Harbour station to catch a normal 4CEP class train, I was informed that due to an incident at Haslemere, the train would be re-routed via Eastleigh but that the journey to London would take about the same time because after Portsmouth and Southsea, it would be going non stop to Waterloo. And certainly once past Eastleigh it did; I don't think I've ever been that fast before in a 4CEP.

Approaching the first station after we left the normal route, the station starter signal was showing red, meaning that we would have to stop, but as we were going very slowly on the approach to it, I could hear very audibly the station public address system announcing that the train was going to Salisbury (or something similar), obviously relating to the train that was expected and not our special. Our train guard hearing this and realising that passengers waiting on the station would think that announcement referred to us, jumped from our barely moving train, ran alongside it and shouted to them "not this train please," or words to that effect. However at that precise moment the signal changed to yellow and the train accelerated, leaving the guard on the platform.

I believe the rules state that if a train comes to a complete stop, the driver must wait for a starting signal from the guard before proceeding, but our train didn't actually stop, so the driver was quite within his rights just to continue. At the next station we stopped for about ten minutes waiting for the guard, who I saw arriving by car. The poor chap had done what he thought best in the circumstances, but how embarrassing for him, and at Waterloo he told me so. I tried to cheer him up by saying that I realised what he was trying to do.

I had just bought one of those new fangled toys called a video camera, and was keen to film some buses at Newport and also some scenes on the last leg of the train journey from Guildford to Reigate.

The trains used on that route were diesel multiple units (DMUs) and, if the driver left his curtain up, quite nice trains for videoing from as you could then see the track ahead, and on this occasion he had. Being a first class ticket holder, and the only one, I took up the best position, the opposite side to the driver, and started filming immediately we left Guildford.

Our train was an 'all stations', the first being Shalford, whereat the driver's cab door opened, and the driver peered through with the question "Can you see all right, do you want to come in here and do it?" Well! He didn't have to ask twice, I didn't want to hurt his feelings, so I joined him.

It turned out he was a driving instructor, and the conversation got around to what did I do, and had I ever driven a train. Actually I had, twice, once an ordinary 4EPB in a depot and the second occasion was a 'Thumper' between Crowborough and Buxted. 'Thumper' is the nickname given to an electro diesel multiple unit because of the way it thumps when under power. The gearbox on the DMUs is similar to a Routemaster, and he asked what did I think of his gear-changes, explaining that the gear changes are to be made at specified engine revolutions which are displayed on a rev. counter.

I replied that I thought he was letting the revs drop too far, and in doing so lost some valuable speed, whereupon he got out of the seat and said, "You have a go, I'm an instructor so will keep an eye on you." After a few changes he understood what I meant.

He then taught me how to stop the train with what I believe were vacuum assisted brakes, with words like, "Don't load them up too much they are a bit slow to bite, just overdo it a bit then immediately back them off, otherwise they lock up." As we were an all stations train I got a lot of practice. I left at Reigate after having one of the most enjoyable days in my life.

RT 1530 the ex-Chiswick skid bus was bought by Westlink, and was repainted by B.E.L. at Willesden. It is seen here alongside my 1963 Mini which has also just received a repaint. But not by B.E.L. *Author*

London Transport's BL class of 90 vehicles were Bristol LH-type buses slightly modified for London Transport requirements. The training schools of London United and London Northern saw a use for them as training vehicles, but not as they currently stood. To replicate a fully-automatic bus, their semi-automatic transmission would have to be modified to fully-automatic. B.E.L. got the contract to do the modification and I was the project manager. The system chosen was the CAV 551, the very same that was being implemented on the refurbished RML and DMS transmission modifications.

The system gave throttle dip between gear changes, as it was thought this method gave a smoother change and was less of a strain on the incoming gear band. It had a few 'funnies' that still catch people out. The most notorious is that throttle is not possible in neutral with the vehicle stationary after a gear has been used. It is only available when first started up, and this is to allow the air to be built up quickly. If needed later to build up air quickly, then it is necessary to re-sequence the bus.

My first test drive was in BL 36, a Holloway bus fitted with coach style seats, and had a carpeted floor, which really made a difference to quietening the vehicle. There was one very important thing I noticed about the gearbox, and that was the length of time it held on to a gear after the gear lever was moved out of a gear. This was very similar, but a lot worse than on the RMCs; this being most noticeable when one went from 1st to reverse. The new selected gear was almost immediately present, but it hadn't released the previous one; the bus just rocked back and forward, i.e., trying to go in two directions at once.

The CAV 551 automatic control system is a Microprocessor based system, which means you can't just take the top off and twiddle the appropriate potentiometer to change a characteristic. If my memory is correct, to set up the characteristics, a clever piece of test gear called an 'emulator' was used. It was housed in an attaché case, and replaced the 551 for the set up, allowing the parameters to be adjusted and chosen as necessary.

When satisfied you then plugged the 551's processor chip into the emulator and 'burnt' the data to that processor. The processor chip was then installed in the 551. Generally the initial settings were the theoretical ones; these being modified by actual road tests. Our first chore was to reduce the time it took for a gear to drop out, and this was done by fitting what is known as "quick dump valves". These devices allow the air to exhaust quickly but have very little effect on the incoming time, not quite the same effect as varying the "restrictor" size. They are a very good idea and I can't understand why they are not universally used – probably cost.

The two training schools though wanted different facilities, and different manual over-ride functions. One wanted the vehicle to always start in 1st gear and there to be a "hold gear" position on the gear lever. The other wanted a system similar to the RM's, but to start in 1st and automatically sequence up, but with the ability to be over-ridden (provided the road speed was correct) by moving the gear lever to one of the other positions. Obviously the two variants had different styles of gear selector, and these we modified ourselves. The general mechanical state of some examples of the buses was appalling. Most had problems with the rather complicated two-alternator charging system, where quite often one had been disconnected, some engines had no guts at all, many had a tendency to stall if you stopped quickly. This particular problem was often because they had been fitted with the wrong fluid flywheel. An RM one will fit, but it creates more drag at tick-over, and a poorly set fuel pump doesn't help either. Bill Cottrell, who we've come across before at Holloway garage, was the only person I have met who could adjust these pumps properly, and he did it "by ear".

What the wonderful fitter had done was to connect the air pipes to the wrong gears, with the 3rd gear air pipe feeding 1st gear and vice-versa. In total we modified about fourteen BLs, but not like that.

The Voith company had become very impressed with the quality of our repairs, and appeared to be content that we furthered our customer base on their products. One very lucrative customer for us was West Midlands Passenger Transport Executive. This company had probably the second largest fleet of Metrobuses in the country, and was willing to entrust us to do their gear panel overhaul work. Its large overhaul works on the outskirts of Birmingham at Erdington reminded me a bit of the old Chiswick works, as they seemed to tackle everything. But like Chiswick they later reduced their product range, and eventually moved to a smaller facility in Walsall.

Business at B.E.L. had its highs and lows. During a low, some of the heavy machinery was sold to the 'highest bidder'; but we never knew who that was. Then a few months later when work picked up, it was realised that we shouldn't have got rid of it, so replacement was sought, found and bought. This replacement was the same one as sold earlier, and probably bought for a lot more than it was sold for – an excellent example of asset stripping. We knew it was the same machine because it still had the LT asset number on it; no one had even bothered to remove it.

In December 1992, due to what many consider poor management, B.E.L. went into receivership, and was offered for sale, but no-one came forward. It was thought that a potential buyer could be Richard Branson and someone actually phoned his office and managed to speak to him. It turned out that he was very aware of the state of B.E.L. but said all his money was ear-marked for other ventures.

The whole episode was a shame and downright disgusting. At the outset of privatisation, the company had been handed all those contacts for work, expertise, and goodwill literally on a plate, and could have sewn up most of the country, dealing with all kinds of road vehicle maintenance, but didn't have the ability (or will) to make it work. There was a common belief that there was no intention of making it a success.

On the morning of the last day, 22nd January 1993, I was in the sales

133

office, and Shon Laird appeared. He had asked why no-one would talk to him, and didn't like it when someone said that we all felt let down by his and his management colleagues' actions.

The work staff had put their lives and souls into trying to make it a success. They had endured three changes of company ownership, moving premises, lost their staff passes, and the state of their pension fund was repeatably being questioned by articles in the *Financial Times*. Most of all, they had lost their personal dignity from being proud of working for what were the best repair establishments in the country – London Transport's Bus Overhaul Works. Amen.

This partly demolished building was once Chiswick's development block and main offices.

After the buildings at Chiswick between the main factory and Chiswick High Road had been closed, it was often put to use as a film set. Here we see fake building facades on the left and a bus stop for a scene for 'The Bill'. On this occasion the corridors and offices for the vacated office block were also used for a chase sequence. *Author*